DRIVING THE VoTE

FOR

WOMEN

AN AMERICAN JOURNEY FOR SUFFRAGE

Jeryl R. Schriever

APPLEWOOD BOOKS

Published by Applewood Books, an imprint of Arcadia Publishing.

For a complete list of books currently available,
please visit us at www.applewoodbooks.com

ISBN 978-1-4290-3040-3

Manufactured in the USA

CONTENTS

For Alex: friend to Saxon drivers everywhere

"PLEASE SHUT OFF YOUR MOTOR, OR GET AWAY FROM HERE," NELL ASKED THE DRIVER OF AN AUTOMOBILE, WHO HAD STOPPED HIS MACHINE BESIDE THE LITTLE SUFFRAGE GOLDEN FLYER.

THE DRIVER SHUT OFF HIS MOTOR.

Author's Notes

My husband, Alex Huppé, bought his first brass-era car in 2010, a 1915 Saxon four-cylinder roadster. Neither of us had ever heard of a Saxon before, but it was a cute little car and ran well enough to take on a Horseless Carriage Club of America tour in Berks County, Pennsylvania. It became clear from the start that touring with this car would always lead to questions. Everyone had heard of Ford Model Ts, but a Saxon? A what?

Longtime Saxon gurus in the Pacific Northwest Elliot Fletcher and Walter Prichard told Alex the story of Alice and Nell. Alex passed on the tale. Curiosity got me. I searched the internet, but few specifics emerged. If they were the first two women to drive across the country and back, why wasn't there more written about them? Being an amateur genealogist, I found some of Alice's family and asked if they had any "papers" from the trip. Alice's great-granddaughter, Bonney Thom, sent some family information but knew little about the 1916 road trip. Days spent searching newspaper archive sites revealed a truly great story.

In 2013 I wrote an article for the *Horseless Carriage Gazette* as the Horseless Carriage Club was looking for stories about women drivers. Due to this article, Mara Rockliff, a children's picture book author, contacted me. Mara was researching the same adventure for an upcoming book, and we began trading information. In August of 2014, Mara and her family came to visit us at our home in Maine. We took lots of photos, and Mara learned how to crank the Saxon and drive it through the blueberry field. Her children's book, *Around America to Win the Vote,* was published shortly after that visit.

I continued researching. In 2019, with the one hundredth anniversary of the Nineteenth Amendment approaching, Seal Cove Auto Museum near Bar Harbor, Maine, was planning a show: *Engines of Change.* It was the perfect time to reintroduce the story of Alice and Nell and the Golden Flyer.

By this time Alex and I had five Saxons and lots—and lots—of parts. The running cars consisted of two four-cylinder roadsters, two six-cylinder touring cars, and one six-cylinder roadster. With the museum show being planned, we volunteered to re-create the Golden Flyer.

Time to gather the needed parts. A spare chassis in the barn had an intact but nonfunctional engine. Rusty roadster parts purchased out of a basement in Connecticut a few years earlier were placed on a trailer that we could roll in and out of the barn. We had an old seat, a dashboard, a steering wheel, and assorted Saxon bits. The metal parts required hours of sanding rust and smoothing. This was accomplished in the driveway. We joked that it was good that the lighting in the museum could be adjusted so the imperfections would not be noticed by most. The seat went to the house to be dealt with later. An area craftsman, George Sprowl, fabricated the cabin floor from the rusted original.

With only black-and-white photos to work with, we had to determine the makeup of "golden" for ourselves. Using charts from automotive colors of the time and comparing white lettering in contrast to "gold" options in a black/white format in Photoshop, we came up with a mix that was most likely a close match.

With the Rustoleum paint mixed and a spray gun attached to the compressor, the Golden Flyer metal pieces rose like the phoenix from the dust. With the help of neighbors, the body was placed on the chassis. The dashboard was sanded and covered in fabric as in the original. The gauges cleaned and reinserted. The steering wheel made to look new. Interestingly, when the old material on the seat was removed so the springs could be retied and new stuffing and fabric attached, there was a small swatch of golden yellow paint on the wood frame behind the passenger's side back. A yellow exactly like the color we had painted the car. Could this possibly be the "real" Golden Flyer?

The newly homemade Flyer was delivered to Seal Cove Auto Museum in the fall along with other period items we had gathered: typewriter, camera, sewing machine. The Alice and Nell story was edited for the museum show. The chief mechanic at the museum, Peter Brown, with a bit of Alex's advice on Saxon priming cups, got the engine to roar to life after at least fifty years of sitting idle. The Saxon now belongs to Seal Cove and is a popular stop for children who have read the story of the Saxon through Mara's book. They are encouraged to sit in the car if they want.

As presented here, this chronicle of Alice Burke and Nell Richardson's journey is far from complete. Told through Alice's diary and supplemented by hundreds of newspaper reports, it tells only part of the tale. Perhaps there are letters out there that the suffragists wrote home, thank-you notes that were written to hosts, complaints they sent to road crews. Certainly, there are many photos in family albums that are marked "unknown *suffragettes* in our town, 1916." Should you find such things in your own attic archive, please send the information along. The story as told here, I'm sure, is just the beginning.

Jeryl Schriever

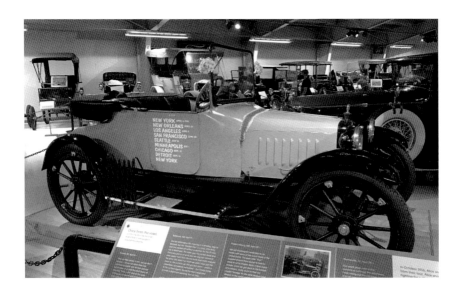

The Golden Flyer at Seal Cove Auto Museum, Seal Cove, Maine

Nell Richardson, passenger, and Alice Burke, pilot of the Golden Flyer,
April, 1916, New York. *Library of Congress*

Foreword

In 1916 Woodrow Wilson was president, Pancho Villa terrorized the southern border states, World War One was raging in Europe, and most women in America wanted the vote.

The fight for suffrage had reached a fevered pitch. Competing women's organizations supported various forms of political activism: marches, pickets, protests, lobbying, newspapers, conventions. Alice Paul's organization, the National Woman's Party, was more militant and worked toward a constitutional amendment following the tactics of British suffragettes. The National American Woman Suffrage Association (NAWSA), led by Carrie Chapman Catt, opposed Paul's militant tactics and preferred a state-by-state campaign of petitions and lobbying.

Though many western states had already granted women universal suffrage, other states only allowed women the vote in limited measure, and other states not at all. To muddy the waters there were arguments regarding temperance, race, and feminism.

The early automobile was part of this drive for change. With its advent, United States suffragists were able to travel farther afield to promote their cause. Many of the roads were rough, but women were determined to share their message of equality and fairness.

In this atmosphere, Alice Snitjer Burke, 39, and Nell Richardson, 25, took off on an epic road trip in a Saxon roadster for "the cause." Supported in tour planning by NAWSA at every stop of their journey, they planned to promote the idea of a woman's right to the vote by speaking to crowds large and small, indoors or out, from a podium or standing on the seat of their car.

Alice was an experienced driver. In 1915 she undertook a two-month tour around New York in *Victory 1915*, a yellow four-cylinder Saxon roadster with Olive Jones, principal of the Disciplinary School for Delinquent Boys of New York. The two embraced warm receptions and endured thrown rotten eggs.

For the 1916 tour, the trip would be harder and longer. Much longer.

Once again, a yellow Saxon roadster was chosen for the trip. As the

Saxon Motor Car Company was promoting its vehicles as inexpensive to buy, economical to run, and "easy enough for a woman to drive," it made sense to use the possibility of a successful trip as an advertising tool. Saxon supplied the car and agreed to aid in the trip whenever and wherever possible. In exchange, the ladies would sing the praises of the little car.

As Saxon provided the car, NAWSA provided the planning. The route was designed for about 100 miles a day with overnight stays hosted by local suffrage organizations. Alice and Nell would speak at every stop, distributing literature and speaking to the crowds. The local Saxon dealership would wash the mud off the car and deal with mechanics as needed.

Though the Saxon was a standard roadster, there were some optional extras: a trunk attached to the rear; tires noted as "heavy duty"; additional lamps attached to provide light during evening outdoor speeches. Items they managed to fit into the car in addition to clothes: a sewing machine, a typewriter, a fireless cooker, a camera, literature, rain gear, car parts, tire chains, and maps. Nell made white slipcovers for the seats to coordinate with their yellow-and-white dresses with embroidered waistbands.

In twenty-six weeks, Alice and Nell covered 10,700 miles over some of the worst roads in America, a country that had yet no national highway system, just a patchwork of local roads. In doing so, they became the first two women to drive across the country and back.

Much of the route can be followed today by reading the newspaper accounts and following period maps. Early in the trip, Alice wrote daily accounts in the form of a "Diary of the Golden Flier," published in the *Boston Globe* and the *New York Tribune*. Later, the trip was documented in local newspapers along the route. Many of the odometer readings presented are educated guesses based on the distances and mileage stated. The state maps reproduced here were created by the Department of the Interior and dated 1915.

Following is the story of two women and a cat touring the country in the Golden Flyer. It is also the story of Saxon Motor Car, America's early roads, and the United States in 1916.

Department of the Interior wall map of the USA produced in 1915. Scanned for use throughout this story, tour stops have been added. *Property of the author*

Nell Richardson and Alice Burke at the christening of the Golden Flyer, Columbus Circle, New York City, April 6, 1916. *Library of Congress*

NEW YORK CITY

THURSDAY, APRIL 6, 1916

NATIONAL AMERICAN WOMAN SUFFRAGE ASSOCIATION (NAWSA) HEADQUARTERS, 171 MADISON AVENUE, NYC

Though it was not specifically reported, Alice Burke and Nell Richardson most likely checked in with the NAWSA staff on the morning of April 6 and received their most recent tour schedule. The NAWSA ladies had placed banners on the car's sides and flowers in its vases. A photographer took publicity shots. Just before eleven, Alice gave the Golden Flyer[1] a single crank and the Saxon was ready to go.

As they pulled out onto Madison Avenue a roar of approval came from the crowd. For almost an hour they drove a long circuitous route to Columbus Circle via Washington Square, Fifth Avenue, and Broadway. Arriving at the circle they were surrounded by folks asking questions and offering advice. Good wishes were everywhere.

At noon the ceremony began.

New York Tribune

SUFFRAGE FLIER SPEEDS ON WAY.

CHRISTENED WITH GASOLENE, IT SWINGS ON FIRST LAP OF 15,000 MILES

With three evening dresses in their tire trunk and seven suffrage speeches in their heads, for lack of room to carry them elsewhere, the suffrage "fliers" started yesterday on their 15,000 mile automobile trip to the coast and back. The "Golden Flier" is the tiniest thing in the automobile line that was ever seen on Broadway. It looked like a little yellow ant scuttling off through the crowds of limousines and auto trucks which lined the streets yesterday.

Mrs. Alice S Burke, the chauffeur only smiled cheerfully when her friends made disparaging remarks about her car.

"We are going through April mud and Arizona desert," she said. "We wouldn't get 10 miles with one of those Pullman cars. This little baby will trot right along regardless of mud and mountains."

The "baby" was christened with due ceremony, promptly on the stroke of 12, at Columbus Circle. Mrs. Carrie Chapman Catt, president of the National Women's Suffrage Association, under whose auspices the automobile trip is being made, broke a pint bottle of gasoline over the radiator.

"BABY" IS CHRISTENED

Twice the precious fluid defied the national president. Her first blow made a big dent in the shining new yellow hood. Mrs. Burke started to groan, then clapped her hands quickly over her mouth.

"Sh——" whispered her partner, "we'll keep that dent and show it to all the folks down south, telling them that Mrs. Catt did that with her own hands."

The proceedings were interrupted by anguished cries from the "movie" men to wait until they had their machines in working order. Mrs. Catt smiled good-naturedly.

"This whole country takes orders from the movies," she murmured.

Finally the bottle was broken, the smell of gasoline greeted every waiting nostril...[2]

At 2:00 P.M. it was time to go. Nell was in place in the passenger seat. As Alice turned to get in the car, a teary-eyed woman rushed to give her a last-minute hug and at the same moment thrust a $10 gold piece into her palm. Alice hesitated a moment then gave a quick lift of her skirt edge—and perhaps a glimpse of hosiery—and whisked the coin out of sight.[3]

...and amid the tooting of half a 100 horns and the cheers of the traffic police the little yellow "baby" swung around the circle on the first lap of a long trip. At the 42nd St. ferry the suffragists kissed the travelers goodbye, and Mrs. Burke divided her bunches of jonquils. George Outler, president of the Good Government Club of the 17th Assembly District, presented each traveler with a new penny for luck.

The first stop was scheduled for Trenton. After that the route lies through Maryland, Virginia, Texas, Arizona, California, Washington, Montana, Illinois, and Ohio. The travelers expect to reach home again about the first of July.

The two autoists expect to be entertained in every town by local suffragists. Down through the South where suffragists are scarce and timid, their arrival will be little short of a sensation.

Both of the travelers have seven suffrage speeches ready to spring at a moment's notice on any crowd that may gather to watch them eat their lunch or mend a tire. As both are experienced campaigners, the national officers feel no trepidation about sending them forth to make up as many more new speeches as the South may demand.[4]

The Saxon Motor Car Company

The Saxon Motor Car Company was incorporated in 1913 in Detroit by automotive genius Hugh Chalmers but it was Harry Ford, Detroit's other Mr. Ford, that turned the company into a success. The first Saxon came off the line in 1914. By 1916 Saxon was America's eighth largest automaker.

The Golden Flyer was a $395 Saxon two-seat runabout. It had a four-cylinder Continental engine and a three-speed inline standard transmission. Boasting impressive fuel economy, 35 mpg, and oil usage—it only used a quart of oil every 125 miles—it was marketed to women, farmers, and businessmen with the promise of economy, ease of operation, and durability. Saxon Motors proclaimed: "America Needs Men With Cars!"

As Saxon had sponsored the suffrage trip Alice took in 1915 around New York, it was logical that Alice might ask, or Saxon might volunteer, to use a Saxon on this trip as well. As a marketing device, if the car could make it the whole way around the country, and driven by a woman no less, the publicity would be well worth the expense.

With its great success, company expansion followed. Unfortunately, bad timing led to the company's downfall. The recession of the early 1920s hit Saxon Motor Car Company hard. The company floundered in Ypsilanti and ultimately filed for bankruptcy in 1922.

NEW JERSEY

TRENTON

APPROXIMATELY 67 MILES TRAVELED

By telegram to the *New York Tribune*

"GOLDEN FLIER" IN TRENTON; ENDS FIRST LEG OF TRIP

TRENTON, N.J. APRIL 6—"The Golden Flier,"...arrived in Trenton at 7 o'clock tonight. The women were escorted by representatives of an automobile company as far as Trenton. From this city they will proceed alone. Although the roads between New York and Trenton were strange to the suffrage motorists, they made the trip without an adverse incident.[5]

Boston Daily Globe

DIARY OF THE GOLDEN FLIER

BY MRS. ALICE S BURKE

They say New Jersey is anti-, but we don't believe it, for our run down here was positively buoyant, with farmers coming out to wave at us and the small towns all shouting "hello, suffs" and all the autos running up alongside with a friendly toot and a grin for our little yellow youngster.

Only one anti- did we see, and that was a horse—a solemn old thing whose world had been upset enough by automobiles without putting women in 'em I suppose. He stood right in the middle of a narrow road and refused to let us by. If he could have talked he would have chanted that woman's place is in the home: but he needed no words, for his determined stand was eloquent enough.

The farmer atop the wagon was completely ashamed of him.

"Don't know what ails the old fool," he apologized, "Ain't generally so cussed. Gidap, Pete!"

Peter, however, remained firm.

Miss Richardson suggested that he did not approve of women suffrage. The farmer grinned.

"'Tain't because he ain't been trained to it then," he submitted. "My daughter's got a badge and belongs to the league in town."

Finally, of course, Pete's objections were overcome and we were permitted to go on, after we had made suffrage speeches suited to the equine understanding and had tied a yellow daffodil rakishly over his left ear.

At Princeton we were met by a large delegation, and the fact that they had mistaken two large trucks painted a suffrage yellow for the "Golden Flier" did not spoil the party at all. "Where's the rest of the machine?" they asked. "This is just the headlight, isn't it?"[6]

PENNSYLVANIA & DELAWARE

DAY 2: FRIDAY, APRIL 7, 1916
TRENTON TO PHILADELPHIA TO WILMINGTON, DE
APPROXIMATELY 132 MILES TRAVELED

Alice and Nell left Trenton at 8:00 A.M. They were finally on their own. No car dealership escort. Just the two of them in their Golden Flyer Saxon.

When they arrived in Philadelphia after a 35-mile ride, they were met by a contingent from the Women Suffrage party. The Pennsylvania ladies were driving their own cars along Northeast Boulevard and came out to escort the Golden Flyer down Broad Street to City Plaza for a mass meeting. After introductions, Alice explained their mission, their hopes, and of course the Golden Flyer.

After a dinner they drove the 32 miles to Wilmington, Delaware.

Gettysburg Compiler
Suffragists of Philadelphia, who, with others of the state, will attend the suffrage demonstrations at the political conventions, were the first to open their traveling expense fund, by issuing an appeal to women to forego costly Easter bonnets and contribute the money saved towards taking delegates westward.[7]

Philadelphia Inquirer
The extra car lights of the Golden Flyer "were to illuminate the dark places of the land...and to demand of the coming National Democratic and Republican Conventions the endorsement of the principle of equal suffrage. If possible, it was said, they would try to heal the split between the Nationals and Congressional Unionists and get them to hit like a football team upon the National Conventions not for two or three things at once, but for the Susan B. Anthony amendment and nothing else."

"It is the intention to ask for a plank endorsing the principle of suffrage, leading all free to work for national and state suffrage as heretofore. If these two great conventions can be brought to endorse suffrage to this extent, the path will be made much easier. "Through its Congressional Committee the national will prepare the plank to be adopted. Men have already been found to introduce it and to fight for it on the floor of each convention. Hearings will be asked as usual before the Resolutions Committees. Each convention city will see great and dignified demonstrations.

"Candidates for elections as delegates should be visited before the primaries and asked to state their positions with regard to such a plank. Each county chairman should send a deputation to interview the delegates nominated from her Congressional district and to make an appeal for their support of such a plank."[8]

The local Delaware newspaper, the *Evening Journal*, reported that the ladies created quite a stir among the Wilmington population as they arrived late in the afternoon. Met at the intersection of 29th and Market Streets by a delegation of Delaware suffragists in seven decorated autos, the Delaware Equal Suffrage Association and the Wilmington Equal Suffrage Association whisked Alice and Nell into town giving them a brief tour before stopping at the City Hall Plaza for an open air meeting. Other local officials where there to greet them and extended warm welcomes. After being introduced, the ladies took turns inviting the audience to check out the little yellow car and explaining their mission.

Over the thousands of miles and multitudes of audiences that would follow, Nell and Alice planned to select the best prepared speeches to use after judging the audience. In states that favored prohibition the ladies would bring that issue into their talks. In the 'wet' regions they would, of course, avoid prohibition.

"In states where women already had the right to vote they planned to talk of the need of a Federal amendment enfranchising women. For the states without equal suffrage the audience would be told to tackle the problem from the state angle.[9]

DAY 3: SATURDAY, APRIL 8, 1916
WILMINGTON, DE TO BALTIMORE, MD
APPROXIMATELY 246 MILES TRAVELED

Boston Daily Globe
DIARY OF THE GOLDEN FLIER
BY MRS. ALICE S BURKE

BALTIMORE, APRIL 8—We left Wilmington this morning in a blinding, raging blizzard, but the "Golden Flyer" is a plucky little thing and she started off without a murmur for the 79-mile trip to Baltimore. The snow was five inches deep and there was plenty of wind, but we dug our raincoats and rubber hats from the tire trunk and really enjoyed the drive. We liked it so much we didn't even put the cover or the curtains up. We got lost once under a snowflake, somebody insinuated—but finally came to the surface again, found the main road, and arrived in Baltimore panting, but on time.

We saw our first peep of green grass at Perryville, Del, which was a bright spot in our young lives and a slap in the face of the blizzard. At Newark, Delaware, we stopped at the railroad station to send a telegram and found ourselves immediately surrounded by a crowd who peered and looked and gazed and stared but said nothing. Finally one of them more enterprising than the rest, spoke up:

"Are you the suffragettes that we've been readin' so much about?" he asked. Are you touring the country?

"We are that." we replied.

"Well say, that's clever, ain't it? Goin' clear to Washington?"

"Farther than that."

"South?"

"South and West and North and East." we answered.

Gee-minee! California?"

"Yes."

He paused, lost in wonder. The rest of them, too, stared at us as if we were creatures of another world.

"I wish we could take every one of you along," I said. "Fine trip," they chorused. "well, we can read about it anyway. G'by, ma-am. Yes'm. Goodbye. Good luck!"[10]

AUTO DEALERS TO ACT ON GAS PRICES

Gasoline, prime necessity of motorists, after advancing steadily to prices never before dreamed of, has in the last three days advanced to 26 cents a gallon retail.

It is probable that some concerted action will be taken by garage men and dealers in motor supplies in the

Roanoke Times (Roanoke, VA), Tuesday January 25, 1916

Early Gas Stations

In 1916, gas stations, as we know them today, were not as common. Instead, early automobile owners often purchased gasoline from general stores, pharmacies, or even hardware stores that had a supply of fuel. Some cities also had curbside pumps where individuals could fill their gas tanks. As the number of automobiles increased, dedicated gas stations began to emerge.

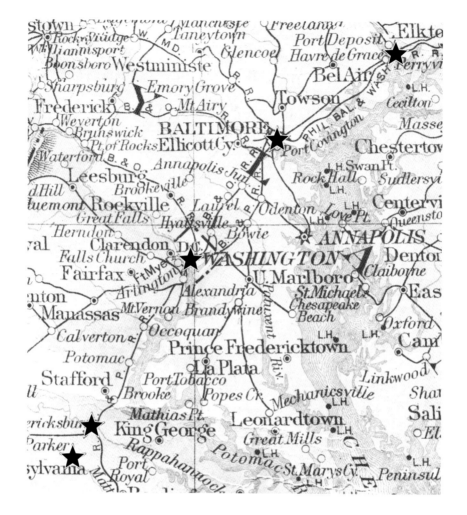

MARYLAND

DAY 3: SATURDAY, APRIL 8, 1916

BALTIMORE, MD

Baltimore Sun
The little "Yellow Catt" chugged into Baltimore about 2:15 o'clock yesterday afternoon, totally unescorted but still bravely running after plowing through the mud and slush between Baltimore and Wilmington. Gone glimmering was the triumphal entry into the city, with a rentinue of 50 cars bringing up the rear; gone was the big open-air meeting at Park and Lexington streets; gone was the jovial

demonstration scheduled for the exterior of the new headquarters of the Equal Suffrage League, 705 Cathedral Street.

Weather, of course. But the "golden flyer" and its occupants...are bearing throughout the United States...were undaunted, and they entered into the jollity of the housewarming with all the enthusiasm in the world.

"After all," they laughed. "The picture men were on the watchout for us so you see we were expected![11]

DAY 4: SUNDAY, APRIL 9, 1916
BALTIMORE TO WASHINGTON, DC
APPROXIMATELY 285 MILES TRAVELED

Boston Daily Globe
DIARY OF THE GOLDEN FLIER

ON THE ROAD, APRIL 9—We've just left Baltimore, where we had a fine reception last night. The hostesses said it would be all right for us to wear our road clothes, but when we fished out of the recesses of the machine two chiffon frocks with tulle scarfs and corsage bouquets, they changed their minds.

This very minute we stopped for gasoline and were forced to give a demonstration of how our little car works. All the men wanted to see inside her, so we waited a while and let them explore to their hearts' content. If you can't win a man by oratory, you can by machinery, sometimes.[12]

IF YOU CAN'T WIN A MAN BY ORATORY,
YOU CAN BY MACHINERY, SOMETIMES.

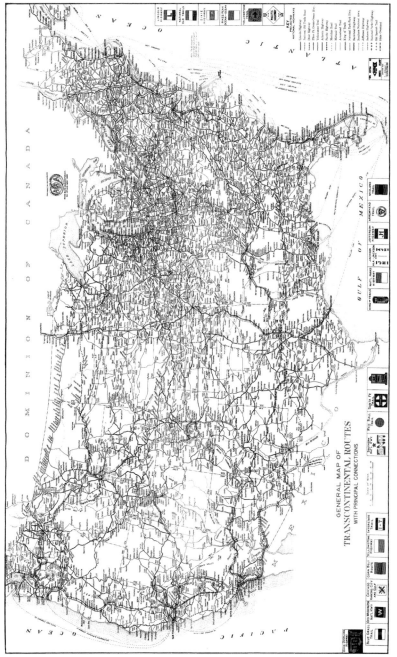

US map produced by the American Automobile Association, 1918, showing the transcontinental routes *Library of Congress*

WASHINGToN, DC & VIRGINIA

DAYS 5 & 6: MONDAY, APRIL 10 AND TUESDAY, APRIL 11

WASHINGTON, DC, TO FREDERICKSBURG, VA
APPROXIMATELY 338 MILES

Boston Daily Globe
DIARY OF THE GOLDEN FLIER
BY MRS. ALICE S BURKE

We left Washington yesterday to do battle with some of the worst roads in the United States. The poor little "Flier" hopped around from bump to hole to creek to rut to stream, fairly a-bob every minute. Once we got stuck in the bottom of a stream, really stuck so that we couldn't budge. As she sank deeper and deeper in the sand and the water kept coming up higher and higher, we became worried and jumped into the stream—icy cold, because it comes from springs above—and cranked and cranked and cranked our arms nearly off.

"Votes for women," said Miss Richardson, by way of a cheer, while I cranked.

"I believe I'll join the good roads campaign instead." I answered grimly.

Finally, when we saw we could not get the "Flier" out of her grounding, we walked a quarter of a mile with water streaming from our clothes and got a chain and several neighbors. We all set to and pulled and tugged and at last got her a few inches. But a few inches was not enough, so we shouted with joy when a big six-cylinder came easing around the head of the road, and soon we were lifted out and on our eventful way again. The going was fairly good for a while, when suddenly we dropped into more mud and our front lights blinked out at the same moment. We now had only a searchlight to illuminate that mud road. Our cranking exercise made us ravenously hungry so we devoured the candy that our New York friends had put in the car like small boys.[13]

[The ladies] "were compelled by the conditions of the highway to wire Washington for assistance. D. S. Ferguson of the AAA joined them. As Alice drove slowly through the darkness Mr. Ferguson walked ahead in the glare of the little car's big searchlight, and with a long pole took soundings as might the watch in the bow of a ship

State of the Roads

Many of the complaints voiced by Alice and Nell during the 1916 trip involved road conditions. Alice is often heard saying that when the campaign for women suffrage is done, she would join the Good Roads Movement.

The story of America's modern roads begins with the bicycle. As bicycles became increasingly popular, their enthusiasts began advocating for better road conditions. The roads of the time were predominantly dirt, which turned muddy during rain and dusty in dry weather. Plank roads were tried but proved less than satisfactory.

This dissatisfaction with the roads laid the foundation for the Good Roads Movement. Initiated in the 1880s, the movement emphasized the economic, social, and cultural benefits of improved roads. Better roads meant better access to markets for farmers, increased mobility for the general public, and overall economic growth. The movement was soon led by automobile enthusiasts rather than bicyclists.

The Yellowstone Trail Association was formed in 1912. It did not build roads but lobbied at the grassroots level and provided local communities information regarding construction and maintaining roads. Its route ran through the northern tier of the United States from Massachusetts to Washington. The Lincoln Highway was also conceived in 1912. Its 1913 route ran through thirteen states from New York to California. The Good Roads Movement caught the attention of Woodrow Wilson, who in 1916 signed the Federal Aid Road Act, which included a national highway plan and federal funding.

By 1919 the projected national highway included not only the Lincoln Highway and the Yellowstone Trail but also the National Old Trails Road, Dixie Highway, Pikes Peak-Ocean to Ocean Highway, Atlantic Highway, Pacific Highway, Meridian Road, Midland Trail, Arrowhead Trail, King of Trails, National Park to Park Highway, Bankhead Highway, Southern National Highway, Jefferson Highway, Jackson Highway, National Parks Highway, Old Spanish Trail, and Dixie Overland.

and called back instructions on how to navigate over the shoals. Even with help, the car got stuck in the mud and there it stayed until 5:30 A.M. when a pair of mules were driven to the rescue."[14]

"Everybody we passed along the way was stuck, which encouraged us." [This] lap of journey between Washington and Fredericksburg consumed many hours and the suffrage car was thrown out of its schedule some 24 hours by bad roads."[15]

DAY 7: WEDNESDAY, APRIL 12, 1916
FREDERICKSBURG–SPOTSYLVANIA–RICHMOND, VA
APPROXIMATELY 407 MILES

Boston Daily Globe
DIARY OF THE GOLDEN FLIER

RICHMOND. VA, APRIL 12—We've had women audiences and men crowds around the Golden Flier, but this morning in little Spottsylvania [sic] we were welcomed by 400 children who came scampering eagerly to see the infant motor car. They were given an extra recess when we pulled in.

Though we really shouldn't have stopped for anything but a much-needed drink of water from the old town pump, they clamored so, those 400 dancing prancing young Americans, that we couldn't refuse. And when we had finished we could hardly get away. They hung on all over the car and trailed us until we had a regular Pied Piper's following. I even had to promise picture postal cards to one energetic youth for his "c'lection" before he would depart from his post of honor by the wheel.

The Virginia roads are really pretty bad, but we have soft air, wild flowers, birds and butterflies, which is a great deal in the life of a touring suffragist; and we are correspondingly grateful.[16]

They arrived in Richmond shortly before 6:00 P.M. and went immediately to work.

San Jose Mercury News

At the corner of Broad and Sixth streets…Mrs Burke kept the crowd under the spell of her magnetism for more than an hour. Whether the men who stopped by on their way up Broad Street to hear her were in favor of suffrage or not they were decidedly in favor of the little woman who answered them. Even the roughest man present—and there were some that did not leave the traditional Virginia impression on the visitors—gave up in the end.

It was not so much a question of women's rights as it was a question of human rights. Anti-suffragists willing to vote twice at the dictation of their good wives caved in with Mrs. Burke's arguments. The very femininity of her methods captured the crowd. Now and then a 'boozer' from a nearby saloon stopped to scoff and remained to pray—at least smile indulgently. He simply couldn't help it.

Mrs Burke handed some hot shots, many of which could have been parried with great success by the proverbial "Philadelphia lawyer," but few of which the 'multitude' was capable of answering. Nobody cared whether she got the best of it or not. Men with hat awry walked up to the cannonade and were toppled over. They came up grinning good-naturedly, and remained, to tell somebody else to shut up.

As she concluded her address Mrs. Burke said—speaking of her automobile—now watch the little darling go by you. The man who had been chiefly conquered because he had been chiefly offensive, gathered the remaining intelligence of his "Three Feathers" and shamefully said, "Which darling? after which somebody shoved him into the darkness of the outside circle. He stood by a telephone pole stroking his chin and muttering. Well I'll vote the entire bunch ding-donged if I don't.

Mrs. Burke, as a final touch, captivated her hearers by telling them that her machine "The Golden Flier" was built especially for her and Miss Richardson by the manufacturers at the request of a California dealer. She took away the last impudence of manhood by deliberately chopping a pert sentence to tell the crowd about the machine.

TELLS OF "GOLDEN FLIER" WITH CHARMING WOMANLINESS SHE EXPLAINED THE MOTOR CAR.

Apparently forgetting the heated assault she had made on the same poor man she began to explain to them that she had a typewriter, a sewing machine, every rod and bolt necessary to repair the car, 16 shirtwaists and so many suits in the car. Look, she said, and see if you can tell where they are? Everybody looked. Somebody stole a wildflower, plucked on the side of a country road between Richmond and Fredericksburg, which the visitors had thrust into the trappings of the headlight. It was an early spring goldenrod.

When the machine was ready to start Mrs. Burke got out and cranked it with her own small hands. Half a dozen of the most critical started forward. Everybody wanted to crank it for her yet somehow bashfulness got the best of them.

"When I was a young woman" she said I" but she never finished. The crowd laughed and cheered and nobody could tell her age for the smile she handed that crowd made them stand back as "The Golden Flier" shot past into the night, the little lady at the steering wheel waving a last farewell.[17]

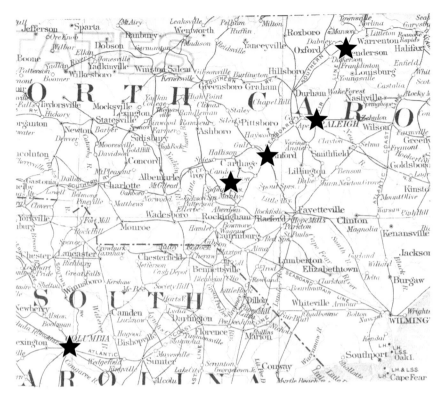

NORTH CAROLINA

Boston Daily Globe

DIARY OF THE GOLDEN FLIER

Left Richmond this morning with fresh daffodils in the vases, good luck slogans and tags tied on to the banner poles, and jars of homemade pickles tucked in the bottom of the car. One timid little woman had whispered to us that the garage men were anti, but the flier must have converted them over night, for it was the garage men who put the daffies in when we weren't looking—nice things!

At Petersburg, the Virginia Automobile Club offered us the hospitality of the club and made us members. They also persuaded us to take a longer route to Henderson as the other road was full of dangerous sharp curved and steep hills, but at that we couldn't make Henderson until today so we spent last night in Clarksville at the town's leading hotel.[18]

Everything (Raleigh, NC)

A large audience gathered in the Senate Chamber of the capitol Thursday evening to hear Mrs. Alice Burke and Miss Nell Richardson, New York suffragists, out on a long automobile tour of the United States in the interest of woman suffrage, heard instead an interesting and very timely address by Chief Justice Walter Clark. The women, who were experiencing something of the sorrows as well as the joys of automobile travel, failed to arrive in their "Golden Flier." Instead, came a telegram from Clarksville saying they had been delayed on account of the roads and would arrive sometime on Friday.[19]

DAY 9: FRIDAY, APRIL 14, 1916
CLARKSVILLE–HENDERSON–RALEIGH–SANFORD
APPROXIMATELY 623 MILES TRAVELED

Since the Thursday Raleigh meeting had taken place without them—and quite successfully—Nell and Alice decided to continue on their journey after a luncheon at the Yarborough Hotel and try to catch up with their schedule.

Boston Daily Globe
DIARY OF THE GOLDEN FLIER

SANFORD, APRIL 14—We left Clarksville early this morning, hoping for good roads, but after leaving Raleigh, about noon, we came upon all kinds of trouble. First we suddenly found ourselves running right into a big hole where a bridge had once been, and we pulled up the car just as her front wheels were about to roll over. We got out, made a danger fence of some poles for the benefit of other motorists who would come along, and then went around through a field. Next we ran into a mud strip, and lost half an hour sounding the mud puddles for shallow ones. We got safely over, and before we knew it we were in the mud again, this time stuck for sure. Out came the chains and into the yellow sticky clay we jumped and finally got the little Flier out, after plastering our clean clothes with mud. Next we had sand, heavy and wet, but we landed after a slow 130 miles in a country hotel in Sanford.[20]

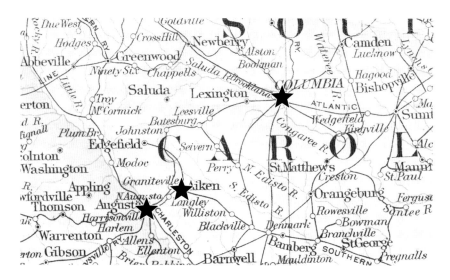

SOUTH CAROLINA

DAY 10: SATURDAY, APRIL 15, 1916
SANFORD TO COLUMBIA, SC
APPROXIMATELY 795 MILES

Boston Daily Globe
DIARY OF THE GOLDEN FLIER

COLUMBIA, SC—We left Sanford [Friday] morning at 6:30. We had ordered the car for 6 o'clock, but had to watch the squirrels until the garage was open, for the negro man forgot to wake up. We had to run 35 miles to Pinehurst for breakfast, and then we made a bee line for Columbia, trying our best to get back on the schedule. The roads were very sandy and heavy and kept up running all day at a steady pull. The country reminded me of the sage brush country of the west, sand belts, trees burnt to the ground, only a few green twigs, and the ground purpling with Johnny Jumpups. This we had for miles and miles.

Suddenly we rounded a corner, climbed a hill and landed in a beautiful fresh green town which was certainly an oasis in our desert. We stopped for a minute or two to ask a few questions and right away had a crowd of men around the car, so we had an informal meeting, and when we drove off they all called after us: "Meet you at the convention in St. Louis!" Sounded like real action to us.[21]

DAY 11: SUNDAY, APRIL 16, 1916
COLUMBIA–AIKEN–AUGUSTA, GA
APPROXIMATELY 871 MILES

Boston Daily Globe
DIARY OF THE GOLDEN FLIER

Mules! What is the psychology of those long-eared, blinking animals that move so slowly off to the side when an automobile comes along, and then jump over the road and nearly create a riot when you pull up alongside? This is what happens every time without fail. They look you over, seem satisfied, and then either back into a ditch or jump over a fence. The drivers don't seem to mind, though being used to the temperamental vagaries of mules. A horse is either frightened or he isn't, but a mule is and isn't frightened all at once.

We went up slowly toward a white mule that was drawing a long wagon and he seemed perfectly serene when suddenly he turned to his right and jumped wildly over a five-foot embankment. For an instant we had a vision of the old white mule with his ears laid back flat, his tail flying out straight behind, and a long thin wagon in the air with a negro clutching on. Then the mule, wagon and driver struck ground right side up, and with no damage done except to the King's English, which suffered a bit when the driver told the mule just what he thought of him.

The Carolinas are the Summer land of the long leaf pine. These wonderful trees are abundant here and from their idly swaying leaves comes an aromatic sweetness that is indescribably fragrant.

The dogwood is tempting too. We stopped and gathered some to decorate the car yesterday afternoon, and had just finished and were on our way again when over the bend of the hill came a big touring car with dozens of "Votes for Women" banners, and we were escorted into Columbia. From Friday morning to Saturday at 7 we had run 315 miles. The little baby motor car has been true to us. We can't blame her when she gets stuck in the mud.[22]

THE 1915 AUTOMOBILE
Blue Books
"STANDARD ROAD GUIDE OF AMERICA"

COVER THE ENTIRE
UNITED STATES AND SOUTHERN CANADA

Volume 1—New York and Canada.
Volume 2—New England and Maritime Provinces.
Volume 3—New Jersey, Pennsylvania and the Southeast.
Volume 4—The Middle Western States.
Volume 5—Mississippi River to the Pacific Coast.
Volume 6—Pacific Coast Automobile Blue Book (Calif., Ore., Wash. and B. C.)

$2.50 PER VOLUME

Blue Book Touring Bureau at the Entire Disposal of Any Owner of
1915 Book for Touring Information of Any Kind, Free of Charge.
Located at Both New York and Chicago Offices.

The Automobile Blue Book

Before the age of GPS and digital maps, navigating America's roads, particularly for early automobile enthusiasts, was a challenging endeavor. The solution came in the form of printed guidebooks, with the Automobile Blue Book being a notable example.

The Automobile Blue Book emerged in the early twentieth century as a critical guide for motorists navigating the nascent American roadways. With the automotive industry in its infancy and road infrastructure still developing, reliable routes and accurate information were indispensable for drivers.

The Blue Book provided comprehensive, detailed directions for a multitude of routes across the country. Beyond mere cartography, it often detailed road conditions, suggested speeds, and indicated points of interest. This made it not just a navigational tool, but also a travel companion, offering insights into landmarks, towns, and services along the way.

Further enriching its value, the Blue Book also listed essential services, including repair shops, fuel stations, and accommodations that welcomed motorists—a crucial feature in an era when not all establishments were equipped to cater to the needs of automobile travelers.

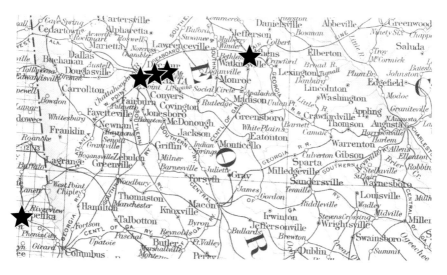

GEORGIA

DAY 12: MONDAY, APRIL 17, 1916
AUGUSTA

New York Tribune

GOLDEN FLIER STARTLES SOUTH

AUGUSTA, GA, APRIL 17—The town of Aiken, Ga, certainly put itself on our suffrage map today. We weren't scheduled to go through there, but the Aiken women had telephoned and wired so insistingly and enthusiastically along our route that we did go and had a perfectly rousing time. We had a street meeting. We met Aiken's "first" and had a wonderful yellow luncheon. Everybody in the whole town was out, and we take off our bonnets to Aiken as a lively little place.

We felt like real society ladies in Augusta this afternoon when they took us to the Country Club where we could rest a while on the big porches. We had to do some coaxing too to get our street meeting here, but we finally persuaded the women to let us try it.

We were all glad we did try it afterward, for we had 500 men who made us talk until we were so hoarse we couldn't make a sound. Every time we would stop they would ask questions, we would answer and then the speech would be on again. We had another meeting in the hotel that night and went to bed pretty well fagged.[23]

The *Augusta Chronicle* reported that the 8:30 meeting at the Albion Hotel hosted by the Equal Suffrage Party was to be a 'charming program' with short speeches and that the public was cordially invited. A story often told by Alice made it into print. "I was to speak before a Danish political club in New York, whose country allows women to vote, you know. But I entered the room the entire club arose and remained standing while I made my 10-minute talk. It hardly seems that they have lost their respect of women, does it?"[24]

DAY 13: TUESDAY, APRIL 18, 1916
AUGUSTA TO ATHENS
APPROXIMATELY 966 MILES

Boston Daily Globe
DIARY OF THE GOLDEN FLIER

ATHENS, APRIL 18—The blue book said that at the foot of a high hill we would run into a deep ford, and naturally we thought it would be a young river and kept our weather eye out for it. But, dear me, all fords are alike it seems—small, harmless, and not to be worried about.

We felt foolish this morning when the time changed an hour and we didn't know about it. I felt like a shoplifter when the clerk in the small town hotel where we stopped for lunch at 10 minutes of 12 raised his eyebrows at us and remarked that luncheon would not be served for an hour and 10 minutes yet, as breakfast was hardly over.

But this afternoon we had a circus, and I mean literally and not in the slang phrase, when I say that. For we were running slowly along the road when we suddenly found ourselves in the middle of a circus parade, red wagon, elephants and all, and the whole roadside lined up with people who had come miles to see it.

The chance was too good to be lost, so we quickly hoisted the banners, selected a place right behind the calliope and attached ourselves to that parade, tooting the horn and throwing suffrage literature out of the car on both sides. It was fine fun, and the country people thought we were all one, vowing that "last year the circus didn't have that little yellow car with women in it."

Athens is a lovely old historical place. We were met as usual and escorted all over the city, visiting the University of Georgia and passing dozens of antebellum homes, pillared and stately.[25]

DAY 14: WEDNESDAY, APRIL 19, 1916
ATHENS–STONE MOUNTAIN–DECATUR
APPROXIMATELY 1,034 MILES TRAVELED

Boston Daily Globe
DIARY OF THE GOLDEN FLIER

STONE MOUNTAIN, GA—We stopped here for lunch and a rest by the wayside. Miss Richardson is finishing up a dress she started in Pennsylvania for it will be two hours before we need to start for Decatur, where the Atlanta suffragists are to meet us. Stone Mountain is an interesting geological structure, a single enormous boulder, perpendicular, and a thousand feet high. The Daughters of the Confederacy propose to cut a great hall out of stones, setting up figures of some of the greatest Southern heroes. Gutzon Borglum has been engaged to execute this remarkable piece of work, and the undertaking will cost $2,000,000.[26]

DAY 15: THURSDAY, APRIL 20, 1916
DECATUR TO ATLANTA
APPROXIMATELY 1,042 MILES TRAVELED

Boston Daily Globe
DIARY OF THE GOLDEN FLIER

ATLANTA—The Atlanta women gave us a wonderful surprise party, coming with 15 cars to Decatur and simply crowding the old Courthouse steps to greet us. The wife of the Mayor of Atlanta was there, the president of the State Suffrage organization with about 75 other women, and it was one grand rally.

It was election day in Decatur and we caught the men in just the right frame of mind, especially the candidates, who of course were most enthusiastic and made speeches in our behalf. After much speechmaking and picture taking and interviewing, etc, we started off for Atlanta. We had a big interested meeting here last night, a luncheon today, and another meeting tonight.

The more we see of Southern men, the more we feel that the Southern women are going to have the vote pretty soon, for as soon as you remove from the Southern man's mind the impression that voting will coarsen their women you have removed his only objection. Suffrage in the South does not seem to be the opposition of corrupt politics as it is in the North.[27]

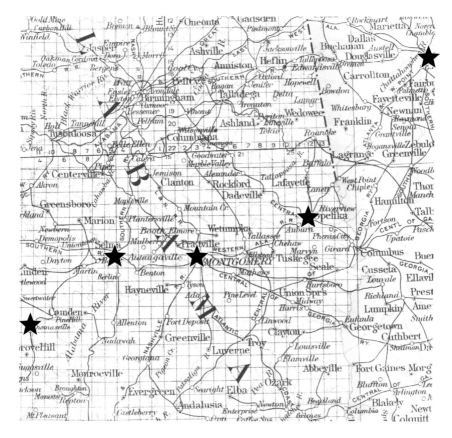

ALABAMA

ATLANTA TO MONTGOMERY, AL

APPROXIMATELY 1,207 MILES TRAVELED

Birmingham News

During the past week the "Flier" has left its golden wake in Alabama. It reached Montgomery Friday, and was met by a delegation of suffragists on the outskirts of the city and escorted to the Capitol, where an open-air meeting was held. Mrs. Burke and Miss Richardson were also entertained at a garden party....

The "Golden Flier" is one of the means the Association has taken to stimulate and arouse suffragists all over the United States in their interest in the conventions and the suffrage plank.[28]

DAY 17: SATURDAY, APRIL 22, 1916
MONTGOMERY–OPELIKA–AUBURN

On Saturday, Alice and Nell moved on to Opelika and Auburn, where a joint suffrage auto parade was held in their honor.[29]

Montgomery Advertiser
NOTED SUFFRAGISTS CARRY DRESSES AND TYPEWRITER IN YELLOW "BABY SAXON" CAR.
MRS. BURKE COOKS, REPAIRS AUTOMOBILE, MAKES
STREET SPEECHES AND WORKS FOR WOMANS SUFFRAGE.
To a crowd of perhaps two hundred women in the lawn of the YWCC [Young Women's Christian Council] Mrs. Alice Burke and Miss Nell Richardson told why women should all work for women's suffrage. They were introduced by Dr. M. B. Kirkpatrick, who says he makes speeches for and against suffrage, being able to give people anything they like in the way of talk.

Gutzon Borglum

Stone Mountain in Georgia is a massive granite outcrop and was intended to feature a sculpture of Confederate leaders Robert E. Lee, Stonewall Jackson, and Jefferson Davis.

Born in 1867 in Idaho, Gutzon Borglum had background in art and sculpture, as his father was a wood-carver. He studied in San Francisco and Paris and traveled through Europe. In his early years he was involved in social causes, and his art often reflected his political beliefs. Gutzon worked on Stone Mountain from 1915 to 1925, but due to artistic and financial disputes with the project's backers, he left before its completion. His work involved creating models and preliminary carvings, but the final carving of the Confederate leaders was completed by other artists after his departure.

Borglum's involvement with Stone Mountain was a significant chapter in his career, and even though he did not finish the project, it provided him with valuable experience and skills that he later applied to his more famous work at Mount Rushmore.

Miss Richardson told of their trip from New York to Montgomery. She said they had met with courtesy in all southern cities and that they had experienced but one accident. That was when it became necessary to ford a stream. The car got stuck and the only way to start the engine was to wade into almost ice cold water. After a struggle, another automobile arrived and pulled the "little yellow Saxon" to high, dry land.

In towns where they were not scheduled to stop, Miss Richardson said that men urged them to give Street speeches and tell them all about women suffrage, what they had done and what it all meant. "And this," she said, "was in the South where we had been warned against the awful conservatism we would have to encounter." Only the utmost friendliessness [sic] had been shown them, Miss Richardson explained and that the "conservatism" was found only among a few individuals.

"The trouble is," said Miss Richardson, "that if we don't keep persistently, everlastingly and constantly at it, the legislators will think we are not sincere and that this woman suffrage is only a spasm or a fad which will pass off when a new one can be found to take its place. Women want to be part of the government and it is only by voting that they can be a part. Men, not only in the South, but throughout the entire country, say they have us on a pedestal. It is a funny pedestal they keep us on when they allow longshoreman to go to the polls, some sober, some intoxicated, some ignorant and some not knowing why or what they are voting for; some foreigners unable to read and write and some more of them traitors to our country and have their say and making of laws governing us. This condition exists in many eastern and Southern States and the women who are supposed to be on a pedestal, must abide by the laws partially made by these people while they, the women, sit idly by without a voice in any governmental matter."

Miss Richardson said that women did not want to be masculine, they did not want to rule men. All they wanted was simple justice.

Mrs. Burke followed Miss Richardson and presented a map of the yellow states, which means suffrage states and the black states, meaning that women were still considered, more or less, a chattel and had absolutely no choice in any legal matters. This map showed the entire west a solid yellow meaning that the women of those states vote on all questions the same as men. It showed the South with the exception of Louisiana and Mississippi, entirely black, and that women could vote on nothing whatever.

"In the next presidential election," said Mrs. Burke, "women had better look out for there will be 4 million women in the west, voting for president and for all other government officials and the west bids fair to get most anything they want.

"Alabama has some of the worst laws of any state in the union," she continued, "for in this state the father is the guardian of the child and the mother has nothing to say whatever if the father cares to exercise his right. He can will away an unborn child, he can, prior to his death, appoint a guardian other than the mother of the child and if the woman works he can draw her wages. If she is able to save by putting away nickels and dimes, a few dollars in a year, the husband could demand that savings and if she refuses, he can get the money by law.

"There are three million children and nine million women in the United States and they are working under conditions which they cannot improve because they are not organized and if they were organized it would do them no good without the vote. Men's organizations would do them no good without the vote but they have that vote and so the politicians take note of what they want.

"If the men suffer, then we want to suffer, if the men have laws to protect them, then we want laws to protect us, if the men have peace, then we want peace. We want to be man's partner, as a partner and also as an individual. This is supposed to be a country by the people, for the people and of the people, but in reality, or legally, it is a country of the people by and for half the people."

AS SOON AS YOU REMOVE FROM THE SOUTHERN MAN'S MIND THE IMPRESSION THAT VOTING WILL COARSEN THEIR WOMEN YOU HAVE REMOVED HIS ONLY OBJECTION.

Following the speeches the YWCA served tea, wafers, stuffed dates and mints to the ladies who attended the meeting. It was the Easter Lily Tea, an annual event that the YWCA took this occasion to entertain the suffragists.

At 5 o'clock Mrs. Burke, Mrs. Richardson and the majority of the women attending the first two speeches joined another crowd at Oak Park where two more talks were given.

Both Mrs. Burke and Miss Richardson are small women weighing, perhaps 110 to 115 pounds. They are sunburned but declare they are strong and perfectly able to stand the trip which they will make entirely in their yellow Saxon driven by Mrs. Burke. Taxation without representation was the theme used in the talk made by Miss Richardson at an open air suffrage meeting held Saturday evening at eight o'clock at Court Square.

Mrs. Snitjer Burke with whom Miss Richardson is traveling, followed her with an argument on the reason why suffrage should be granted to the women of America.

"The Southern men," said Mrs. Burke, after her talk, "are far more chivalrous than the men of the north and we have been accorded every courtesy that we could wish for on our trip south."[30]

DAY 18: SUNDAY, APRIL 23, 1916
MONTGOMERY TO SELMA
APPROXIMATELY 1,257 MILES TRAVELED

On Sunday, Alice and Nell made the quick drive to Selma where they spent a quiet Easter.

DAY 19: MONDAY, APRIL 24, 1916
SELMA TO THOMASVILLE, AL
APPROXIMATELY 1,300 MILES

New York Tribune
"DIARY OF THE GOLDEN FLYER"
THOMASVILLE, ALA, APRIL 24—Our spark plugs won a few converts to suffrage this afternoon. I was taking out the old ones, and a lot of men gathered around the car and watched me tug and pull and

finally loosen them, and then put in the new ones. They were pretty curious to see whether I could really do it or not, and seemed a bit surprised that the Flier really would go after the manipulation of feminine hand. But when it was finished they all exclaimed, "Good work, " and one of them added, with true Southern eloquence, that "woman's hand in the machinery of politics might have the same helpful effect."

We posted the notice of our meeting in the postoffice tonight and had about two hundred people around the car.[31]

DAY 20: TUESDAY, APRIL 25, 1916
THOMASVILLE TO MOBILE
APPROXIMATELY 1,417 MILES TRAVELED

New York Tribune
"DIARY OF THE GOLDEN FLYER"

MOBILE—We hardly noticed the bumps and holes to-day, though they were just as bad as usual, for we were passing through a most enchanting country. Blossoming orange groves, avenues of huge live oaks, pecan orchards, sugar plantations, and everything hung with streamers of gray Spanish moss—I could hardly drive the car for looking, looking, looking.

We had three real little "Yellow Kids" here in Mobile to-night; they were the six-year-old daughters of some of the Mobile suffragists, and they were in the automobile parade, dressed in jonquil yellow.

I cannot rid myself of this surprised feeling I have when I see what a real live issue suffrage is even in the most placid, most atmospheric, most traditional Southern town. Suffrage flourishes like a flower under the sunny skies and soft breezes of the South. Everywhere we go the people stick little presents about the car. We have had some very queer things, but the little black cat that a man in Mobile presented is as interesting as anything we have received yet. Bars of chocolate are a favorite gift, and flowers we always get. Pickles and jelly and doughnuts we have always with us.[32]

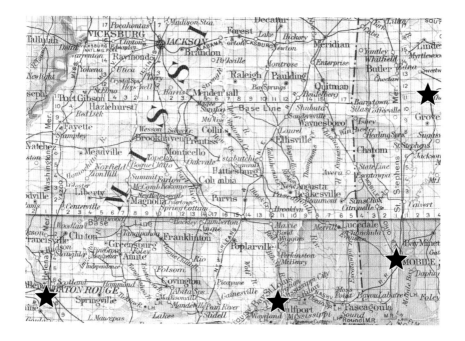

MISSISSIPPI

DAY 21: WEDNESDAY, APRIL 26, 1916
MOBILE, AL TO GULFPORT, MS
APPROXIMATELY 1,494 MILES TRAVELED

New York Tribune
"DIARY OF THE GOLDEN FLYER"
GULFPORT, MISS., APRIL 26—The street crowds were crazy about the St. Louis "Walkless Parade" plans, especially the men, who like the "silent plea" idea. We had a Democrat delegate in our audience to-night, and all the other men of the crowd had lots of fun "pledging" him to help us with our plank on June 14. He good naturedly promised, and they all cheered.[33]

It had been three weeks since Alice and Nell left New York in a sea of daffodils and good wishes. New Orleans was the destination for Thursday but the roads were reported to be bad. They needed to find an alternative route.

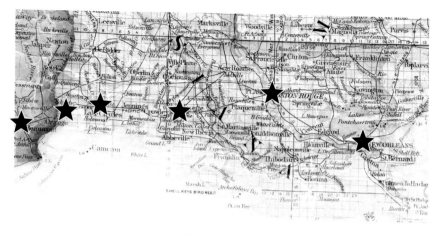

LoUISIANA

New Orleans States

2 SUFFRAGE CRUSADERS AND CAT MASCOT ABOARD YELLOW CAR HERE TODAY

They arrived in New Orleans Thursday morning by train. For the first time during their 15,000 mile trip through "border states" that they had had to ship their car and ride the train a while. Near Gulfport the streams proved no longer fordable and the road mud altogether too deep for the little yellow car.

Life, to two suffrage crusaders is a series of mud puddles, with a creek now and then to relieve the monotony. This, Mrs. Burke confided Thursday evening while the small black kitten climbed up one of her arms and curled up comfortably on her shoulder.

You guessed it—the kitten is the mascot of the expedition. But what you'll have to be told is his name is Saxon, and he wears a yellow ribbon about his neck. "We've had an awful time smuggling him into hotels," said Mrs. Burke. "What do you suppose the management would do now if they knew we had a cat up here? This morning on the train we were miserably afraid the conductor would find out we had him.

"We had to camp out one night because our car stuck fast in a bog," related Mrs. Burke. "The greatest adventures we have had, though, were when we were ferried across streams in South Alabama at the rate of about a half a mile a day. We often were drenched all over, but it wasn't so bad when we knew that tucked away in our waterproof chest were plenty of warm dry things including two evening frocks ready to put on."[34]

DAY 23: FRIDAY, APRIL 28, 1916
NEW ORLEANS TO BATON ROUGE, LA
APPROXIMATELY 1,659 MILES TRAVELED

New York Tribune
"DIARY OF THE GOLDEN FLYER"
Baton Rouge, La. April 29.—We had to ship the car from Gulfport to New Orleans yesterday as the bridges between the two places were all down, and we therefore had our first—and we hope last—train ride of the trip. Ran down here along the Mississippi levee, and though we couldn't see the river from the levee, we were much interested in the rice fields, sugar and cotton plantations and the old Spanish and French plantation houses on the other side. We were late in getting into Baton Rouge because of a broken spring, which snapped when we were in the middle of a stream. We had a dramatic time in the water again—most of our tragedies are staged in midstream, it seems—but after pulling the fender off so it would not rub the tire we finally crawled out and ran along at a snail's pace into Baton Rouge.

We had a moving picture crowd here tonight. The announcement of our meeting had been flashed on the screens of all the moving picture houses in the town about half an hour before, and every movie fan in town accordingly was on the spot when the little Flier appeared. We knew we had the movies to compete against for the interest of that crowd, and were scared to death that our suffrage talks would seem very prosy compared to the thrills of the photoplay, but they were a live crowd and kept firing questions, so that we had at merry time of it, after all.[35]

State Times Advocate (Baton Rouge, LA)
YELLOW ROADSTER ROSTRUM OF SUFFRAGISTS.
WOMEN'S RIGHTS ADVOCATES HARANGUE B R MULTITUDE.
"An interesting and well-mannered not sympathetic audience" heard

Mrs. Alice Burke and Miss Nell Richardson, equal suffrage advocates, plead their cause Friday night in front of the Istrouma hotel, with the little yellow Saxon roadster in which they are touring the United States serving as a rostrum.

Both Mrs. Burke and Miss Richardson spoke Friday night standing on the seat of the little roadster which they had drawn up by the curb in front of the Istrouma hotel. Only one auditor attempted to argue the issues of equal suffrage with the speakers, and as he threatened to become boisterous in driving home his arguments, the police took him away and the meeting proceeded.

The crowd did not seem willing to finance its conversion to championship of women's rights and tuned out considerably when Miss Richardson dismounted from the Saxon to take up a collection. Most of the crowd stayed, however, and heard Mrs. Burke tell of the advances made in other states in the cause of woman suffrage and listened attentively to the exposition of her theories of a government with both men and women taking part in bringing about the reforms necessary for the good of humanity.[36]

DAY 24: SATURDAY, APRIL 29, 1916
BATON ROUGE TO MORGAN CITY, LA
APPROXIMATELY 1,725 MILES TRAVELED

State Times Advocate (Baton Rouge, LA)

After getting their automobile repaired Saturday morning, the two suffragists left for Morgan City their next stopping place. From there they will go to Lake Charles, and then strike out to Texas on their way to the Pacific coast.

"We well [sic] touch the Mexican border four times on our trip to the coast," said Mrs. Burke "and this has caused our friends in New York to become anxious about us. They have tried to dissuade us from [t]aking the southern route to the coast, but we do not think we will have any trouble, though no doubt the Mexicans would consider it quite a feast to capture us because we have been so widely advertised in the United States."[37]

DAY 25: SUNDAY, APRIL 30, 1916
MORGAN CITY, LA

New York Tribune
"DIARY OF THE GOLDEN FLYER,"

MORGAN CITY, LA., APRIL 30—About thirty-five miles out of Morgan City the same spring broke again. It had been poorly mended, and we were absolutely stranded on that swampy Louisiana road. It was sundown, and we were afraid they might have to spend the night there but some obliging Creoles came along, tied us up with firewood and rope, and we plugged along at five miles an hour, stopping also every few minutes to wake up the mules and horses sleeping comfortably on the road. Arrived at the hotel at 12 o'clock, both worn out."[38]

DAY 26: MONDAY, MAY 1, 1916
MORGAN CITY TO RAYNE, LA
APPROXIMATELY 1,813 MILES TRAVELED

New York Tribune
"DIARY OF THE GOLDEN FLYER"

RANGE, LA., MAY 1—We certainly didn't have a very flowery May Day. Left Morgan City this morning, struck a road that was six inches deep in dust, and a perfectly wild wind was blowing the dust up so that we couldn't see three feet in front of the car. We lost the road dozens of times, and even though the Creole farmers were more than anxious to set us straight, their English was inadequate. This afternoon a frightful storm came up, the lightning blazing around the car and the water coming down like a sheet. We simply stumbled upon this little village and aren't a bit sure where we are. Our bed is a queer looking article of furniture, stuffed with dried moss. But feathers and eiderdown and embroidered linen never looked more inviting than this lumpy, hard affair that we're going to rest on to-night.[39]

DAY 27: TUESDAY, MAY 2, 1916
RAYNE TO VINTON, LA
APPROXIMATELY 1,896 MILES TRAVELED

DAY 28: WEDNESDAY, MAY 3, 1916
VINTON TO BEAUMONT, TX VIA TRAIN
APPROXIMATELY 1,936 MILES TRAVELED

What Is Creole?

In places like Louisiana, "Creole" denotes a unique cultural group with European, African, and sometimes Native American ancestry. The Creole culture in Louisiana has its distinct architecture, cuisine, and traditions that arose from this blend of influences.

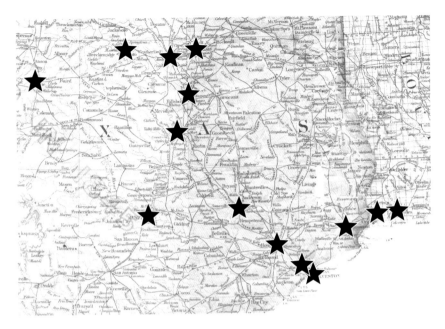

TEXAS

The Houston Post reported that the Golden Flyer was shipped from Vinton, LA to Beaumont, TX, due to bad roads.[40]

New York Tribune
"DIARY OF THE GOLDEN FLYER"

BEAUMONT, TEX., MAY 3—Broken springs and bad roads have kept us overtime in Beaumont, and our schedule is a mangled and torn thing. But Beaumont is very hospitable and we have enjoyed the town hugely. Yesterday we joined in a mock circus with the Rotary Club of Beaumont, and made suffrage speeches between the acts. Last night we went out in machines to Port Arthur and had a big meeting outside a bank. It was pay night at the oil refineries, so we caught the men in large numbers—and good humor. We spoke before three woman's clubs here and have been tead [sic] incessantly. Texas is a good suffrage state. The suffragists have a very fair chance to get their bill through the next Legislature, and as one session is all that is required in Texas it will soon be up to the people here.

We saw the famous Spindletop yesterday, where the first Texas oil was discovered so many years ago.[41]

DAY 29: THURSDAY, MAY 4, 1916
BEAUMONT TO HOUSTON, TX
APPROXIMATELY 2,023 MILES TRAVELED

New York Tribune
"DIARY OF THE GOLDEN FLYER"

HOUSTON, MAY 4—Our first real night of rest since we left New York, April 6, and this because we got here a day ahead of the new schedule. We were received well, however, even the elevator boy in our hotel grinning his welcome.[42]

DAY 31: SATURDAY, MAY 6, 1916
HOUSTON TO TEXAS CITY TO GALVESTON
APPROXIMATELY 2,081 MILES TRAVELED

Stopped at Texas City, a new little oil town, to-day on our way here for a noon meeting. And such weather. Good old sun beating down while we stood in the car and talked parades and let our noses blister and burn and peel, our clothes wilt and our hair sizzle. Yet, they say women are vain and that suffragists are not martyrs! I should advise any young woman who wants rosy cheeks to stand in the sun of Texas City, Tex., for a few brief moments, where a permanent flush is guaranteed.

Galveston is a wonderful city, rebuilt with a fine courage that makes one admire the people extraordinarily.

The Galveston women gave us some very useful gifts to-night, a spade to dig ourselves out of the sand with and canvas bags in which to carry and protect extra cans of water. Apparently we have a desert trip before us.[43]

DAY 32: SUNDAY, MAY 7, 1916
GALVESTON BACK TO HOUSTON
APPROXIMATELY 2,134 MILES TRAVELED

DAY 33: MONDAY, MAY 8, 1916
HOUSTON

We came back to Houston for the scheduled meetings and parade, and will go on to Dallas tomorrow, where the state suffrage convention opens this week. Texas suffragists have arranged for a private car to carry the Texas delegation to the "walkless" parade at St Louis.[44]

Houston Post
COURIERS OF SUFFRAGE SPOKE TO LARGE CROWD
Two Golden Flyer Travelers Talking
From Auto at Noon Hour Monday

Spindletop

The Spindletop story began when Pattillo Higgins, a local business-man, and W. Scott Heywood, a mining engineer, became convinced that the Spindletop Hill, a salt dome, was rich with oil. Despite numerous failed drilling attempts and skepticism from many experts, their persistence eventually paid off.

On January 10, 1901, drilling at the Spindletop site led to a massive gusher, which sprayed oil over 150 feet into the air. Pro-ducing at an initial rate of around 100,000 barrels per day, this well, known as the Lucas Gusher, surpassed the combined output of all the oil wells in the United States at the time. Its discovery signaled the beginning of the Texas oil boom.

Spindletop brought a rush of prospectors and investors to the region, transforming Beaumont from a small town into a bustling city almost overnight. The gusher led to further exploration and the establishment of other oil fields across Texas.

By 1916, Texas had firmly established itself as a major hub in the global oil industry, a reputation that began with the legendary gush at Spindletop. Before its discovery, the American oil industry was primarily situated in the Northeast, with Pennsylvania being a dominant player.

Feline Symbolism & the Suffrage Movement

A cat? Why would anyone want a cat companion on a road trip?

While there are numerous symbols and icons associated with the suffrage movement—purple, white, and green tricolor flags or yellow and blue sashes—one of the lesser-known but nonetheless significant symbols associated with suffrage was the cat.

In the early 20th century, the domestic sphere was traditionally associated with women. Cats, as household pets, were often linked to domesticity and, by extension, to femininity. Antisuffrage propaganda often used cats as a symbol of the domestic duties that women should supposedly adhere to, in contrast to the political arena. One such instance is the portrayal of suffragists as old maids with cats, suggesting that their activism was a result of personal bitterness rather than genuine conviction. The term "pussy cat" was used pejoratively against women, trying to trivialize their efforts.

As is often the case with symbols, they can be reappropriated and transformed. Suffragists began reclaiming the cat imagery. Instead of viewing the cat as a symbol of passive domesticity, they embraced its attributes of independence, agility, and resilience. Cats are known for their autonomous nature, a quality that resonated with women seeking rights and recognition as individuals, not just extensions of their husbands or fathers.

During the suffrage movement, postcards became a popular means of propaganda for both suffragists and their opponents. Cats frequently featured in these postcards. Anti-suffrage postcards might show cats in domestic roles, with captions suggesting that women's place was at home, not at the polling booth. On the other hand, pro-suffrage postcards reclaimed this imagery, showing cats participating in marches or advocating for votes for women, drawing parallels between their independent nature and the suffragist cause.

In some instances, cats were adopted as informal mascots for the suffrage movement. They became a kind of 'silent protester' accompanying women at rallies or events. Their calm and poised demeanor contrasted sharply with the often hysterical portrayal of suffragists by the media, making a silent yet impactful statement.

It is interesting to note the contrast between the symbolism of cats in the suffrage movement and the bulldog, which was often associated with masculinity and politics. While the bulldog represented the political establishment—staunch, resistant to change, and aggressive—the cat symbolized a new, nuanced, and determined form of activism.

The journey of the cat, from a symbol of passive domesticity to one of resilience and autonomy, mirrors the journey of women from the confines of the household to the broader societal and political arena. This transformation underscores the tenacity of the suffrage movement and its ability to reshape narratives in its pursuit of equality.

Miss Nell Richardson and Mrs. Alice S. Burke in suffrage car.

From *The Times*, Shreveport, Louisiana, Thursday, April 13, 1916.
A publicity photo taken before Alice and Nell left New York and used
in many newspapers around the country. *source: newspapers.com*

Mrs. Alice Burke and Miss Nell Richardson, suffragette speakers, both of New York, spoke to a large crowd at Main Street and Texas avenue Monday noon. While speaking they stood on the seat of a small runabout in which they are touring the country.

Talks were made by both ladies and lasted nearly an hour. Mrs. Burke declared that the suffragists would concentrate their work on the republicans and democrats. A suffrage plank has already been placed in the platform of the progressive party.

After the talks, the two couriers in their auto headed a procession of about 20 automobiles through the downtown streets. All the cars were decorated with the suffrage colors.

Mrs. Burke and Miss Richardson left later en route Dallas, to attend the Texas State suffrage convention. It is their plan to then proceed westward to the Pacific coast, returning east via the Northern route.[45]

DAY 34: TUESDAY, MAY 9, 1916
HOUSTON–NAVISOTA–WACO, TX
APPROXIMATELY 2,319 MILES TRAVELED

New York Tribune
"DIARY OF THE GOLDEN FLYER"
WACO, MAY 9—Stopped in Navisota for a noon meeting. Still very hot. I'm sure I shall dream about the white poppy fields we passed to-day, the loveliest sweep of fragrant whiteness one can imagine.[46]

DAY 35: WEDNESDAY, MAY 10, 1916
WACO–MILFORD–DALLAS, TX
APPROXIMATELY 2,519 MILES TRAVELED

Dallas Morning News
"VOTES FOR WOMEN" CAR REACHES DALLAS.
MRS. ALICE BURKE AND MISS RICHARDSON, FAMOUS TRAVELERS, GUESTS
Flying a dust-covered pendant bearing the legend "Votes for Women" the "Golden Flyer," the famous little yellow car which Mrs. Alice Burke and Miss Nell Richardson are making a coast to coast tour for women's suffrage arrived at the Adolphus Hotel at 4:30 o'clock...and

its two travel-stained occupants immediately went up to the Texas Woman Suffrage Association convention in the palm garden of the hotel. And although the day's journey had taken them across deep sands, ruts three feet deep and creeks where the Bridges had washed away—to use their own words—they were not one minute late either. A bystander observed that promptness is one of the characteristics of the "new woman."

"If war broke out tomorrow, we never could get our troops anywhere," Mrs. Burke said. "Between Houston and Waco—our Tuesday's run—we had to go through sand so deep that a mule could not pull out of it, many of the bridges were washed away and the ruts formed by the cakes of mud were fully three feet deep. I believe it was the hardest day we have had since leaving New York on April 6.

"Everywhere we go people stop us on the road and want to know if they can make the trip all right. I tell them they can if they were doing it as work but that they can't just on a pleasure trip. Only 10 percent of the roads we have covered have been good. The worst piece of road we got stuck was just out of Washington, D. C."

Mrs. Burke lives in New York and appeared to be about 25 years old in the flowered organdie dress she was wearing, although she declared she would be 40 on the 16th of the month. Miss Richardson's home is in Winchester, Va. She is 26 years of age. The heavy coats of sunburn which both ladies wore only heightened their youthful appearance.

CAR IS CONSPICUOUS

The canvas covering over the seat of the "Golden Flyer" was covered with names, dates and remarks. "F. O. B." stood out prominently. "New York April 6; New Orleans April 27" were among the legends. The body of the car was also dotted with stickers. The equipment includes a hand sewing machine, a typewriter, a fireless cooker, several canvas bags filled with clothes and a spade donated by the Galveston suffragists. Moving pictures of the trippers were shown in Dallas Tuesday night proceeding their arrival by day.

The itinerant suffragists said that they had found a strong movement for their cause wherever they went. They felt sure Texas would be for suffrage because they had received the largest collections in Houston and Galveston of any places visited. "But of course Dallas will soon head the list," Miss Richardson broke into Mrs. Burke narrative. The funds are sent to the national suffrage organization.

"If the women of the South would only wake up and say they want suffrage they would have no trouble getting it," Mrs. Burke concluded before going to her room to dress for the suffrage banquet.[47]

DAY 36: THURSDAY, MAY 11, 1916
DALLAS

Staying at the Adolphus Hotel in Dallas, a luxurious 22-story hotel completed just three years earlier by beer magnate Adolphus Busch, Alice and Nell could relax a bit. Not only was it a beautiful place to stay but had the advantage of being only three blocks from the Ray Rose Company Saxon dealership so they could keep an eye on the Golden Flier as she was cleansed of her latest road grime.

DAY 37: FRIDAY, MAY 12, 1916
DALLAS TO WACO
APPROXIMATELY 2,519 MILES TRAVELED

New York Tribune
"DIARY OF THE GOLDEN FLYER"
The troops are mobilizing in San Antonio to-day, the very day we should have reached that city, according to the old schedule. We're glad to be out of the danger zone, though it seemed pretty close yesterday at Waco as we watched the troops going on [the] train for the border.

The farmers down here believe in using every bit of ground, even if they do have more of it than anybody else, for one-half of our road yesterday was ploughed and planted with potatoes, the good husbandmen taking advantage of the fact that it was much too soft for travel. I call that thrift.

Yesterday we had a splendid convention mass meeting and last night a huge banquet. We love the parties that we attend on tour, for it's so good to dress up and have things served by courses; the dust of the road and the cracker boxes are not the things we enjoy most.

The little black kitten is suffering as much as we are from the heat but he keeps under a cover, and all we can see around the corner of it is a pink nose and a youthful whisker.[48]

DAY 38: SATURDAY, MAY 13, 1916
WACO TO AUSTIN
APPROXIMATELY 2,623 MILES TRAVELED

El Paso Herald
SUFFRAGE AUTO FAILS TO COME
LOCAL SUFFRAGETTES HAVE DINNER
ANYHOW AND LISTEN TO SPEECHES.

On account of the bad roads below Valentine, the route of the "Golden Flyer," the yellow automobile in which Mrs. Alice Burke and Miss Nell Richardson are traveling from New York city to San Francisco in the interests of women's suffrage, was changed to a more northerly route and so El Paso is not visited by the suffrage speakers. The luncheon, to have been given in their honor by the El Paso Equal Franchise League Friday, was held without the guests in the grill room at the Hotel Sheldon.[49]

DAY 39: SUNDAY, MAY 14, 1916
AUSTIN TRAVELING NORTH

DAY 40: MONDAY, MAY 15, 1916
ARRIVED AT MINERAL WELLS
APPROXIMATELY 2,823 MILES TRAVELED

New York Tribune
"DIARY OF THE GOLDEN FLYER"
MINERAL WELLS, TEX,. MAY 15—We left here once to-day, but thirty miles out the Flyer suddenly stopped dead and I couldn't locate the trouble to save me. Neither could all the other motorists that came along, so we had to submit to the humiliation of being towed back. It turned out to be a broken gear pin. I shall never have any confidence in gear pins again.[50]

DAY 42: WEDNESDAY, MAY 17, 1916
COLORADO, TX
APPROXIMATELY 3,010 MILES TRAVELED

New York Tribune
"DIARY OF THE GOLDEN FLYER"

COLORADO, MAY 17—Not the state, but the very small Texas town of the same name; one of the smallest there is, too. But never mind: we played revival hymns on the parlor organ of our hotel to-night and had the best food we've had since we've been out. Also, we got in on a high school graduation dinner, where all the girls in white dresses and the boys in high, stiff collars told us about their class prophecy and their class picnic, and then permitted us to say a few humble words about our own mission in the world. It was a fine chance to talk about "three times as many women as men graduating from the public schools," for the boys were in the decided minority. Our street meeting was composed mostly of sober faced cowboys and a few Mexicans. I must say we'd feel just as comfortable if the Mexicans would stay in "women's place" whenever we're around.[51]

White Poppies of Texas

The poppies that Alice and Nell observed were probably white prickly poppies, *Argemone albiflora*. When they bloom in Texas en masse they are said to be amazing. They are not only native to Texas but to other parts of the southern US and northern Mexico. The poppies stand out not only for their large petals—four inches across—but also for their distinctive blue-green leaves and thorny stem. Generally about three feet tall, the poppies bloom between March and July.

The plant thrives in disturbed soils, making it common in areas like roadsides, pastures, and other open areas. Its adaptability to the Texas climate, with its hot temperatures and periodic droughts, makes it a staple in the state's diverse wildflower display.

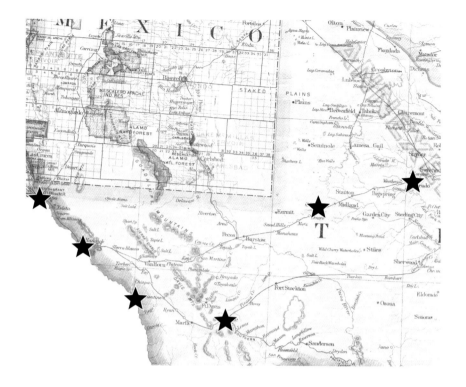

DAY 43: THURSDAY, MAY 18, 1916
COLORADO TO ODESSA, TX
APPROXIMATELY 3,113 MILES TRAVELED

New York Tribune
"DIARY OF THE GOLDEN FLYER"
ODESSA, MAY 18—We got stuck on the prairie for several hours to-day and then were run into by an excited motorist who isn't used to meeting cars. The wind is blowing such a gale that the whole hotel shakes, and the wall paper cracks and rattles and all but blows off the walls.[52]

DAY 44: FRIDAY, MAY 19, 1916
ODESSA TO ALPINE, TX
APPROXIMATELY 3,266 MILES TRAVELED

New York Tribune

"DIARY OF THE GOLDEN FLYER"

ALPINE, MAY 19—We arrived here to-night after a day's travel in clouds of alkali dust and gusts of hot wind. The night does not promise to be entirely peaceful either, as we have orders that "if a whistle blows from the pumping station, rush to the schoolhouse." This means a Mexican raid, and I have visions now of our trying to make away in the Flyer. The streets are patrolled and the Home Guard—armed citizens—are ready and, frankly, we are scared to death. Everybody is cheerful over the danger, though, which is reassuring to timid travelers. The kitten is ill, poor infant, but we are trying to help him along and hoping, too, that this isn't his ninth and last life.[53]

DAY 45: SATURDAY, MAY 20, 1916
ALPINE–VALENTINE–SIERRA BLANCA, TX
APPROXIMATELY 3,400 MILES TRAVELED

El Paso Herald

While press reports state that the "Golden Saxon Flier" with the touring suffragets will not pass through El Paso, G. E. Cavin, of the Western Auto company, is hopeful that the schedule will permit the tourists to visit this city and the fact that a large quantity of mail awaits them here leads to the belief that the "Golden Flier" will be seen here after all.

"Business is getting better every week now," said Tom White, of the Auditorium garage. "Many owners got scared of a Mexican situation and decided to overhaul the old cars instead of buying new ones and that naturally meant more business for the shops."[54]

DAY 46: SUNDAY, MAY 21, 1916
SIERRA BLANCA TO EL PASO, TX
APPROXIMATELY 3,469 MILES TRAVELED

SAXONS HAVE PART IN VILLA CHASE
EL PASO DEALER DONATES CARS TO THE

QUARTERMASTER CORPS.

Saxon motor cars are playing a part in the chase of the United States troops after Pancho Villa, bandit and Mexican revolution leader.

Just as the sturdy race which gave them their name always played a prominent part in the warfare of the British Isles and the northern part of Europe, so are the motor cars giving their best to the service of Uncle Sam on the sluggish Rio Grande. At El Paso, Tex., where a large number of troops have been stationed since the border mobilization in 1913, three Saxon motor cars were sold to United States army officers before the pursuit of Villa and they were used by the officers for trips about the border.

First Lieutenant Guy H. Wyman of the Eighth cavalry is the owner of a Saxon Six and Second Lieutenants Welton M. Modisette and William A. Robarg of the Fifteenth cavalry both have Saxon Four roadsters.

CARS PRESSED INTO SERVICE.

When the United States decided to enter Mexico in pursuit of Villa and the border was thrown into a fever of excitement, these three officers found a practical use for their motor cars in patrol duty and messenger service in and about El Paso. The cars were pressed into service because they cover ground faster than a horse and because the sand and mesquite of the border country offered no obstruction to them.

At the same time F. O. Calvin, Saxon dealer at El Paso, placed three other machines at the service of the government. He took cars from his stock for this purpose and offered them to the army officers. Mr. Calvin hesitated a bit at doing this but finally decided to give them without consulting the factory. When he wired what he had done he had the unqualified approval of H. W. Ford, president and general manager of the Saxon company.

Mr. Ford is a strong believer in preparedness and has himself taken an active interest in the movement for military training in this country. He assured Mr. Calvin that the Saxon company stood ready to help the government and its great task of supplying the flying column of General Pershing.

The cars which were loaned to the army were all Saxons "Sixes" and they have found a ready use in the quartermaster corps. One of them is being used daily by a major of that department and it has traveled hundreds of miles in the last two weeks. The sturdy construction of the Saxon motor cars makes them particularly adaptable to the rough roads and prairies of the border country, according to Mr. Calvin. Their light weight permits them to travel through the sand and their mechanical perfection has given them a reliability that is needed for this sort of work. Except for the motor truck companies there are few motor cars being used by the forces now in Mexico. The country makes them less practical than horses for messenger work. On the border the motor car is feasible and Saxon has its place at the top among the types in use.[55]

El Paso Herald
SUFFRAGETS HERE IN CAR TO HOLD MASS MEETING IN CLEVELAND SQUARE
Speak on Street Corners

Miss Nell Richardson of Virginia and Mrs. Alice Snitjer Burke of New York City, accompanied by their mascot, a little black cat named "Saxon," arrived Sunday night in their Saxon car. "The Golden Flyer," having traveled 3400 miles working for equal suffrage.

Mrs. Burke and Miss Richardson were due in El Paso a week ago but a changed routing delayed their arrival. They are guests of Mrs. A. C. DeGroff at Hotel Orndorff. During the whole of their trip so far, they have not had a puncture nor any engine trouble, but have met with frequent accidents with their springs, and Saturday at Sierra Blanca, the oil pan of the car was torn off by a high center and the travelers were delayed for repairs.

Mrs. Burke and Miss Richardson left New York [in] April, the "Golden Flyer" being christened for the trip by Mrs. Carrie Chapman Catt. The main purpose of the trip is to solicit the aid of all the women of the country for a mammoth demonstration in favor of equal suffrage at St. Louis at the time of the Democratic convention. At this convention, a 'Walkless Parade" will be held. Each side of every street leading to the convention hall will be lined with women uniformly dressed wearing equal suffrage baldricks and carrying suffrage banners and distributing equal suffrage literature while other workers will endeavor to secure the cooperation of the Democratic party leaders for the incorporation of an equal suffrage plank in the patry [sic] platform.

At noon today El Paso heard its first out of doors street corner speeches for equal suffrage. Mrs. Burke and Miss Richardson, in their automobile, addressed crowds on various corners of San Antonio street, talking on reasons why women should have equal citizenship rights with men and the right to vote.

Tonight in Cleveland Square, Mrs. Burke and Miss Richardson will speak on equal suffrage at a public mass meeting at 8 o'clock. John Fielding, jr., will introduce them. Mrs. Burke and Miss Richardson will speak again at Noon Tuesday on the streets of the city.

They will leave Wednesday morning for Deming on their way to California.[56]

El Paso Herald
VOTE HUNTERS HAVE A THRILL.
TOURING SUFFRAGISTS LOSE SLEEP; ARE
SCARED OF THE MEXICAN BANDITS

A little golden colored Saxon roadster created considerable attention on the streets of El Paso this week. This car has gained national fame as the "Golden Flier" and is being used by Mrs. Alice Burke and Miss Nellie Richardson for a tour across America in the interest of "votes for women". After being set right by Mrs. Burke as to the term "suffraget," the auto editor is content to leave aside all subjects of "suffragists" and "suffragets."

The tour tourists have had some unique experiences on the way, but they got their real thrills between El Paso and Alpine. They reached Alpine last Friday night. There was a Mexican "scare" on at the time and when the two women were assigned to rooms on the ground floor of an Alpine hotel they were a little uneasy. They became still more uneasy when they saw men in the lobby carrying businesslike rifles and revolvers. "I didn't take off my clothes or shut my eyes all night, "said Mrs. Burke.

The following day the tourists were met between Alpine and Sierra Blanca by G. E. Cavin, the local Saxon distributor, and his son. They told Mr. Cavin of their experiences at Alpine and he "poopoohed" the idea of there being any danger.

"I really began to feel reassured," said Mrs. Burke, "and then I happened to look into his touring car. Down by Mr. Cavin's feet there were two big rifles which looked as if they were intended more for use than decoration. I asked him why he carried the rifles if there wasn't any danger.

"He went on telling me that there was no danger, but his son spoke up and said that Mr. Cavin had put the rifles handy for if we need them at all, we'll need them darned quick.

"It was very reassuring. I can tell you. We got to Sierra Blanca that night with our nerves somewhat shaken. There we were told that if the school bell was rung during the night, we were to "hike" for the school house. It's needless to tell you that we had mighty little sleep that night.

"I was never so glad for anything in my life as I was to get into El Paso. Everybody here tells us there is nothing to worry about but I think that I prefer my touring a little farther north."[57]

DAY 47: MONDAY, MAY 22, 1916

EL PASO, TX

New York Tribune
"DIARY OF THE GOLDEN FLYER"

EL PASO, TEX., MAY 22—We've been in this delightful cosmopolitan city for several days now, and in spite of patrols and soldiers and war news, we've had splendid suffrage audiences. Had a meeting to-day in a public park, with a most enthusiastic crowd. The town is full of country people all the time who are afraid to stay in the country now, and who come to the city every night to get their night's sleep in safety.

Our trip to El Paso was long and lonely. We didn't see white men for hours and passed many Mexican villages. I don't see how people can live on these hot dry plains. The prairie dogs are the only form of life that has any spirit at all. Whenever we eat luncheon on the road the only shade we can find is the shade the car makes. One week more and we'll be in beautiful California.[58]

El Paso Herald
SOUTH'S CHIVALRY REFUSES VOTE TO WOMEN
Enslaves Children Suffrage Leader Says Nation Can Rise no Higher Than Its Motherhood and That as We Regard Our Mothers, So Will the World Regard Us; Thinks Mothers as Safe With the Ballot as the New Foreigner.

"If men had been as thoughtful of the rights of women as of their own, the country would not be in the present economic condition where men are losing their jobs to women who work for lower wages," said Mrs. Alice Snitjer Burke, in her address on equal suffrage in Cleveland Square Monday night.

"Men have protected themselves by labor organizations and laws stipulating the amount of hours they shall work and the minimum wage they shall receive, but in the states where men only have suffrage, the men have done nothing to lower the hours of a woman's work or standardize her wage, consequently when some firm desires to economize and discharges all its men employees, substituting instead women at half the wages you men howl that the women are taking away your jobs. You men have done it yourself, for if you voters had passed a law granting equal pay for equal work, and the eight hour day law for women as well as for yourselves, these economic conditions would not exist.

THE SOUTH AND CHIVALRY

"We hear a lot from the southern men about their chivalry," continued Mrs. Burke, "and how they do not want their women to be taken off the pedestal upon which they have been placed. But the examples of this chivalry plan result in the known fact that in the southern states are the worst laws concerning women and children on the whole nation. In Georgia the age of consent is as low as 10 years, which is the lowest in the United States.

Worse Than Negro Slavery

"In South Carolina the chivalry of the men permit laws to exist which allows a system of child labor that is worse than the days of negro slavery. The chivalry of the men classes the women of the south, your own mother, wife, sweetheart and sister, with the only three classes prohibited from the right of suffrage—criminals, idiots and imbeciles.

No Right to Ask Why

"No one of you men bother to think how you will vote. You do not ask the immigrant all these questions before permitting him to vote, after he is naturalized; you simply give him the right to vote and let it go at that, yet the immigrant often merely comes over here for a job and has no particularly vital interest in the welfare of the country.

"The women have a vital interest in the welfare of this country for it is our country as much as it is you men's. It is our state, our city and our home, just as much as it is yours.

"Everything we do is affected by laws and we have just as much right to help make the laws that are to govern us as you have.

Women Best Educated

"Women as a class are better educated and more intelligent than men as a class. The annual average of girls who graduate from colleges and high schools is much higher than the percentage of boys."

Mrs. Burke urged her hearers to remember that women were not working to gain the ballot for the purpose of becoming office-holders. She said that they simply wanted their rightful half share in helping make the laws and that men did not realize how much they were losing by not having the women's help. This world was made for men and women together, not simply for one sex or the other.

Nation No Greater than Source

"A nation is no greater than its source," she said. "Surely the source of every nation is motherhood. As a nation regards its mothers so is that nation regarded."

Miss Nell Richardson talked on the work that is being done by the suffrage organizations all through the country and particularly in New York city, to create a favorable interest in suffrage.[59]

DAY 48: TUESDAY, MAY 23, 1916
EL PASO, TX

El Paso Times

SUFFRAGE LEADER TAKES RAP AT MERE MAN IN AUDIENCE

WHEN HE ATTEMPTED TO BE FUNNY, MRS. BURKE PUTS HIM ON "PAN"

Demonstrating her own suffrage argument that women possess sufficient intellect to cope with men, Mrs. Alice Snitzer Burke, of New York City, last night at a suffrage street meeting in Pioneer plaza, met remarks meant to be facetious from men in her audience with quick witted answers that made them ridiculous and which won the audience to her side. After the first few attempts from masculine members of the audience to make Mrs. Burke the butt of suffrage jokes, the raillery subsided.

Mrs. Burke and Mrs. Nell Richardson, the two New York suffrage speakers, drew so large a crowd at a street speech at noon yesterday that the police stopped the speeches because the crowd was blocking traffic. Before the meeting last night, Mrs. Burke sought a place on the curb removed from plate glass windows. "Not because I fear that anything will be thrown, but because the crowds lean against them and occasionally break them," she said.

SPOKE FROM CAR

The two suffragists spoke from the seat of their yellow Saxon roadster, in which they are touring the country in the interest of equal suffrage.

"You men of Texas," commanded Mrs. Burke, "see that your state is the first in the south to have votes for women. Bring pressure to bear on your congressional delegation at Austin, and see that the question is submitted to the voters."

Several of the hearers in the crowd attempted to argue the suffrage question with the two women. The crowds applauded the two, and took their side in every argument. Most of the men withdrew from the crowds at the first opportunity after they had encountered the ready replies of Mrs. Burke and Miss Richardson.

"I love to speak to street crowds," said Mrs. Burke last night. "I know when I speak to people on the street that they are listening to me because they are interested. In speaking to an audience in doors, one always feel that they have to sit through it all and listen, whether they are interested or not."

Miss Richardson did not hesitate to make her crowd behave while she was speaking. "Please shut off your motor, or get away from here," she asked the driver of an automobile, who had stopped his machine beside the little suffrage "Golden Flyer." The driver shut off his motor.

New York campaign

Miss Richardson told of the New York state suffrage campaign of last year, and outlined the methods to be taken by local suffrage advocates in procuring the vote.

Mrs. Burke and Miss Richardson proved to be a revelation to the people of El Paso, who have gotten their idea of the suffrage campaign in the east chiefly from suffragette cartoons. At first, the people of the city were inclined to take their speeches as jokes, and were attracted by the novelty of hearing women speak on the streets. When they saw the seriousness of the two women, and learned the logic of some of their arguments most of those who had come to scoff remained to absorb all they could of the equal franchise movement.

Those who expected the militant, window smashing, brick throwing suffragette were disappointed in the two. Both proved to be women of refinement, well educated, and with the nerve to express their opinions from an automobile on the streets in the face of numerous difficulties.

Mrs. Burke and Miss Richardson intended to leave El Paso yesterday afternoon, but repairs on their automobile, the "Golden Flyer," forced them to remain over until this morning. The street speech last night was not on the regular program, but was made to further their work of advocating equal suffrage.[60]

Suffrage Organizations

The National American Woman Suffrage Association, NAWSA, and the National Woman's Party, NWP, were two prominent organizations in the early twentieth-century US women's suffrage movement, but they had distinct strategies and leadership.

The National American Woman Suffrage Association was founded in 1890. Leaders included Susan B. Anthony, Elizabeth Cady Stanton, and later, Carrie Chapman Catt. NAWSA primarily advocated for suffrage on a state-by-state basis and took a moderate approach. They used lobbying and organized parades and gave public speeches. NAWSA believed that demonstrating women's patriotism and commitment to World War I would help their cause. Alice and Nell belonged to NAWSA.

National Woman's Party was founded by Alice Paul and Lucy Burns in 1916 as a more radical alternative to NAWSA. The NWP adopted militant tactics inspired by the British suffragettes. They picketed the White House, organized hunger strikes, and engaged in civil disobedience. Their focus was on securing a federal amendment for women's suffrage.

As Alice and Nell were driving their historic road trip, they were well aware of which states had already given women the right to vote. In those areas they would urge the population to support those states which were still fighting for enfranchisement. When it came to an amendment to the Constitution to pass, it would need three-quarters of the states to agree.

By 1916, eleven states, mainly in the West, had already granted women full or partial suffrage rights. Alaska as a territory had granted women the right to vote in 1913.

Wyoming (1869); Colorado (1893); Utah (1896); Idaho (1896); Washington (1910); California (1911); Arizona (1912); Kansas (1912); Oregon (1912); Nevada (1914); Montana (1914).

DAY 49: WEDNESDAY, MAY 24, 1916
EL PASO, TX TO DEMING, NM
APPROXIMATELY 3,544 MILES TRAVELED

Detroit Times

The men of the south and west are in favor of suffrage. The Texas men are especially friendly but the ignorance of the woman may hold it back. Women who do not understand what suffrage means shy at the word. They all believe they should have a voice in the schools, playgrounds and all questions pertaining to home and children, but they do not understand that they can never have it without the ballot.[61]

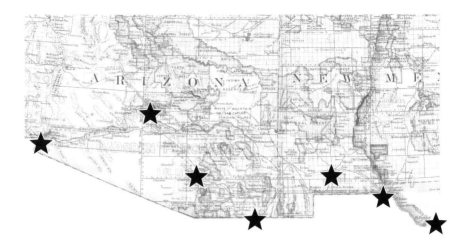

NEW MEXIC & ARIZONA

DAY 50: THURSDAY, MAY 25, 1916
DEMING, NM TO DOUGLAS, AZ
APPROXIMATELY 3,701 MILES TRAVELED

DAY 51: FRIDAY, MAY 26, 1916
DOUGLAS, AZ TO TUCSON, AZ
APPROXIMATELY 3,823 MILES TRAVELED

The welcome in Tucson could be described as "informal." Alice and Nell went to the Chamber of Commerce where the Civic League was in session and at the end spoke briefly about their mission during an informal reception. Part of the lackluster enthusiasm could have been that Alice and Nell represented NAWSA which was considered a rival of the local suffrage group, the Congressional Union for Women's Suffrage. Or, it could be that the perhaps "lack of enthusiasm" was due to the fact that the women of Arizona already had the right to vote. Arizona was the first state they had come to where women were already enfranchised. There was no need for publicity in Arizona.

The Saxon Motor Car company however could use the publicity. The company has been very helpful in aiding in the journey. Not only did Saxon supply the car for this venture but they had been maintaining the Golden Flier along the way. Alice was not naive. She knew that the company was

map obtained for them by the A. A. A. they have already motored through fifteen states; ten more are included in their itinerary. They have held outdoor meetings urging the women of the west to give to their eastern sisters encouragement and support.

They were met in Phoenix by Mrs. Eugene Brady O'Neill, president of the Civic League and foremost among suffrage workers in this country. At eight o'clock last night the little yellow automobile halted at the corner of First and Washington streets and speeches were in order.

The methods of the National Suffrage Association are very different from those of the Congressional Union. Militancy and the Woman's party have no place in the outlined policy of the association.

Tired and dusty on their arrival there were no complaints from either of the suffragists on their arrival. There had been tire trouble and other happenings on the road but "what of it?" was their attitude. As Mrs. Burke went about automobile repairing and Miss Richardson launched into an enthusiastic suffrage talk. She made one realize that the vote does not give woman emancipation.

And with all that there is to do for the cause the principal thing just now is to pass the Susan B Anthony amendment.

In denouncing the Congressional Union, Miss Richardson contrasted the two policies—the N. S. A. and the Union. "We do not believe in choking a thing down the throat of the party in power. We believe in securing or attempting to secure the endorsement of every individual regardless of party affiliations."

Miss Richardson stated she would like to see western women in great numbers at the conventions

"They have told us in the east that you will not stand with us. We want to show them that the western and eastern women are united in this and knowing the significance they place upon the presence of the representatives of the western states we are urging them to go. It will help more than any one thing."

She spoke of the parade of 40,000 suffragists to be held in Chicago suffrage week and of the already famous Walker parade to be held in St. Louis during the other convention. We will be stationed 30,000 strong in front of the hotels where the delegates are located and make a personal appeal for a suffrage plank in the platform. And I hope that every woman voter will make that same appeal to her delegates."

Miss Richardson regretted the conflict between the Congressional Union and the Suffrage Association.

"It proves what the men have said—that women will not stand together."

MRS. ALICE S. BURKE WRESTLES TIRE ADJUSTMENT PROBLEMS AND CONVINCES REPORTER SHE SHOULD AND CAN HAVE THE BALLOT

"What do you need of a credit slip, if you're going to get your tires replaced free on the coast," Mrs. Alice S. Burke, motoring suffragist was asked after she had won a battle over the replacement of a Goodrich tire from the local branch manager.

"I might get stuck at some tank station and need that $4.50 she replied. Mrs. Burke convinced a Republican reporter last evening that she ought to have the right to vote. She did it by finessing the auto men and by bossing them when bossing was necessary. Your average for the afternoon was .750 in points won and lost. And most any team can win with that percentage.

She drove in from Tucson in the "Golden Flyer" a Saxon roadster of a violent yellow hue and a smoothly purring motor. A gift, it was, from the New York Saxon branch. She rode on Goodrich black safeties—also a gift. All the utilities and most of the decorations on the little buzz-buggy were gifts. And they were all secured from New York men. Strange isn't it, that Mrs. Burke has not persuaded the men to give her the vote."

If the opponents of suffrage are all as courteously conquered as the Goodrich man, Mrs. Burke's party will win by attrition.

If the women of the west are as deely [sic] impressed by Mrs. Burke's 1000 percent self reliance as the Republican reporter, her party will win by accretion.

Hunch: Mrs. Burke's party WILL win. May be a long time, though.

It was no use trying to interview the plucky chauffeuse on suffrage. At the first query, she spun out a "line of talk" relating to pet cocks, brake bands, crank cases, high centers, etc. which banished thought of ballots and concentrated attention on mechanical details of which she seemed an absolute "master."

"Arizona roads are the best we have journey over so far." Mrs. Burke was not soft-soaping, for she followed that statement with a minute description of the ills of southern roads.

"I have had two punctures since leaving New York. Mechanical trouble has never been such that I couldn't make temporary reparations on the road in order to reach a garage. High centers sheered my foot brake rod at one place and I "broke" on one wheel for a while and later on the other. I will reach Yuma the day I start out to reach it. How is the road?"[63]

Route 1161 — Phoenix to Yuma, Ariz. — 206.9 m.

MILEAGES
Total Intermed.

Total	Intermed.	
0.0	0.0	**PHOENIX,** Court House on right. Go north on **2nd Ave.**
0.1	0.1	**Van Buren St.;** turn left crossing RR. 1.5 straight through **Cashion** 12.0 crossing RR. at **Coldwater** 14.5 and 23.1.
24.7	24.6	End of road; turn right.
26.4	1.7	**LIBERTY.** Straight ahead.
31.1	4.7	End of road; turn left going straight through **Buckeye** 32.4.
34.6	3.5	End of road; turn left.
35.6	1.0	First 4-corners; turn right.
37.6	2.0	End of road; turn left.
38.1	0.5	First right-hand road; turn right.
39.1	1.0	**PALO VERDE.** Straight ahead fording Hassayampa River 41.7 going straight through **Arlington** 45.6.
49.2	10.1	Right-hand road; turn right with main travel.
91.8	42.6	**AQUA CALIENTE.** Straight ahead passing **Palomas** 103.3.
107.4	15.6	End of road; turn right swinging left just beyond following main travel avoiding all right and left roads. Enter Pass through Castle Dome Mountains 154.8 leaving Pass 157.7.
162.6	55.2	**CASTLE DOME.** Straight ahead avoiding road to left 162.7. Bear right 163.7 and 167.7 avoiding road to right 170.7 and 172.5. Bear left 183.2.
186.1	23.5	Fork; bear right fording Gila River 187.6.
188.3	2.2	**GILA CITY.** Bear right around P. O. going straight through Dome 188.7. **Caution** for sharp turn upgrade 189.5, along RR. grade jogging across same 193.0 and 193.1 avoiding road to the left 193.4.
206.4	18.1	Left-hand branch road; bear left swinging right just beyond at freight depot to center of
206.0	0.5	**YUMA.**

Mile by mile directions for crossing the desert from east to west from the *Automobile Blue Book 1913. Vol 5: Mississippi River to Pacific Coast*, page 933.

Route 1266—Yuma to Phoenix, Ariz.—206.9 m.

Route map, page 947   Reverse route, No. 1161

Follows the course of the Gila River, famous in Pueblo and Aztec history and noted for its ruins of Casa Grande. Adobe, sandy and gravel roads mostly through cactus deserts and over lava beds; good dirt roads near Phoenix.

For the first 21 miles the road runs through a desert region, being very sandy and rough in spots. At Gila City the Gila River must be forded, as the water is usually too low to allow of ferrying. There are two fords and both are approached through a long stretch of very heavy sand. The river is a dangerous one to cross on engine power only and the motorist is strongly advised to obtain a mule team at the store (charge $2.50). For some miles beyond one passes through a picturesque cactus region over good natural roads and smooth lava beds; the scenery is often grand and there are fine mountain panoramas. Good time can be made here, in spite of the numerous dry creek beds which have to be crossed. At about the 49th mile the road is stony and enters a pass in the desert. Once the mountains are crossed there is a fine natural gravel road down-grade to the valley, but after leaving Deep Well the way is stony and the trails are difficult to follow, while there are numerous washouts in the draws all the way to the hot springs of Agua Caliente, where there is a hotel. Lunch can be had here and as a night stop it will do at a pinch. The saline waters of the springs make a most refreshing drink. A succession of trails through lava beds and sandy and gravel cactus deserts follow and dry creeks have to be crossed many times. In spots, however, the road is like a boulevard to Arlington, where one enters the fertile reclamation lands of the country around Phoenix. The latter city is surrounded by a network of irrigation ditches and a variation upon the route here given may have to be made to avoid flooded roads. The motorist should make inquiries in the neighborhood of Cashion.

Advice for crossing the desert from west to east from the *Automobile Blue Book 1913. Vol 5: Mississippi River to Pacific Coast*, page 984.

DESERT

DAY 54: MONDAY, MAY 29, 1916

THE ROAD WEST FROM PHOENIX

Detroit Times

They reached the border of Texas in May, just before the National guard was sent to Mexico and report that conditions there were worse than any northerner imagines. In crossing the desert of Arizona they were often alarmed by stray shots. They declare that many American women were kidnaped by Mexicans in border raids. They passed Mrs. Deemer, who was rushing in an automobile from California to El Paso to assist her son, who had been taken prisoner by the Mexicans.[64]

Starting off from Phoenix on Monday morning the Golden Flyer headed west along the Old Spanish Trail. Shown on the map were the towns of Coldwater, Buckley, Agua Caliente, Palomas scattered along the route. The suffragists most likely were sure they could find services along the way.

They did not. Their friends started to worry when there was no word on Monday night.

DAY 55: TUESDAY, MAY 30, 1916
HEADING TO YUMA
APPROXIMATELY 4,120 MILES TRAVELED

Telegram to Mrs. Helen Gardener in San Diego from Yuma, AZ
WANDERED IN THE DESERT TWO DAYS.
MAKE SAN DIEGO THURSDAY.[65]

Oakland Tribune
"Out of Phoenix we went through our worst mental journey. The horrors of thirst was ever with us, although only once did we suffer, and then not for long.

"Several times we were stuck on this part of the journey through the high centers in the road, which absolutely no motorcar could negotiate.

"We were stuck one place here some distance west of Phoenix, and asked the assistance of some men in a passing vehicle. A little help would have got us over the high center, but these men informed us they were in a hurry and that we could get assistance at a town a short distance back. We could not wait, as we only had about a pint of water left in the car, and started out on foot for the town, which proved to be six miles away.

"That was the longest six miles of our journey. Tired out trying to get the car over the high center, we had hardly enough strength left to plow through the sand a-foot back to the town.[66]

Oregon Daily Journal
"The roads have been bad and we had a great deal of trouble crossing the desert. It is not sand as most people think but dust. Each machine that crosses deepens the track. If you get into a groove the machine gets caught in a rut and must be dug out." (ASB)[67]

Anaconda Standard
"My, but water, or anything that passes for it tastes good on the desert," said Miss Richardson. "We had water in a bag for drinking purposes but the machine went dry and he [sic] had to use it for the radiator.

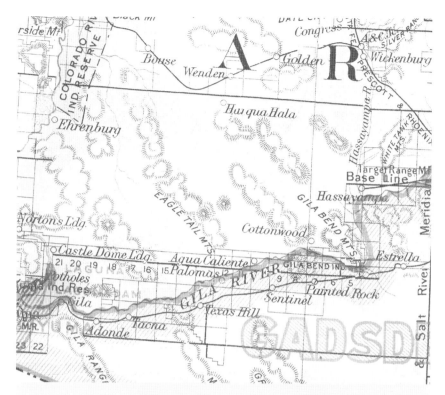

Crossing the Desert

Crossing the American Southwest desert in an automobile in 1916 would have been a challenging undertaking. Most roads weren't paved but were instead dirt tracks, often unmarked. An auto could get stuck on the high center caused by years of wagon usage. Even those roads that were "planked" could be obscured by sand. Rain might make them impassable. The lack of road signs could easily lead to getting lost in the desert's vast expanses.

May in the southwest US can be really hot, adding to the issue of lack of shelter or water or any kind of services. In addition, add the threat of rattlesnakes.

Their destination, Yuma, had also experienced flooding from the Colorado River during the winter, turning the desert's typical hard-packed terrain into muddy, sticky traps. Did the ladies see this? They didn't say.

The descriptions the ladies gave after the trip were the events that feed nightmares.

Then we got lost and by the time we found the trail we were out of water again and had to abandon the machine. We walked seven miles to the next stopping place and there found a hole which the signboard said was a well. We dug into it and found feathers and a dead chicken in the stuff caller [sic] water. Say, but that stuff tasted good. Water on the desert is a funny water. The more you drink of it the more thirsty you get, but it keeps you from dying."

For days the young women traveled along the Mexican border without seeing a white man. They were never molested, though they feared kidnapping because they had been so thoroughly advertised and were afraid that some Mexican bandits might get them and hold them for ransom.

They had to leave the regular trail several times because of war conditions. At one place they passed along the Rio Grande with Mexicans on one side and Americans soldiers on the other, both firing at each other while the automobileists passed between.

"I'd like to see any man do better than we did on this trip," declared Miss Burke."[68]

Finally reaching Yuma with an hour or two to recover from their desert travels, Alice and Nell were ready for the five thousand strong Preparedness Parade in the afternoon. When the preparedness speeches were done, Nell and Alice delivered their suffrage speeches to the large crowd.

CALIFORNIA

DAY 56: WEDNESDAY, MAY 31, 1916
YUMA, AZ TO EL CENTRO, CA

APPROXIMATELY 4,181 MILES TRAVELED

Los Angeles Times, June 1

THEY'RE NOT LOST

New York Society Women Campaigning for
Suffrage are Safe in El Centro, Despite Alarming
Reports That They Were Astray on the Desert

Andrew Baldwin, a representative of the Saxon Motor Sales Company
denied yesterday that [the suffragists] had been lost on the desert
between El Paso and this city.

Although rumors were circulated in this city yesterday that
friends of the two women had not heard from them in nearly a
week, Mr. Baldwin stated that the San Diego Motor Company's
representative received a telephone message yesterday morning from

Mrs. Burke, who said she and Miss Richardson were in El Centro. They are expected to arrive in this city Sunday or Monday.[69]

DAY 57: THURSDAY, JUNE 1, 1916
EL CENTRO, CA

DAY 58: FRIDAY, JUNE 2, 1916
EL CENTRO TO SAN DIEGO
APPROXIMATELY 4,294 MILES TRAVELED

The San Diego Saxon dealer, Howard B. Smith, plus W. P. Creswell met the Golden Flier ladies at El Campo to escort them into the city. Alice and Nell were given the grand sightseeing tour of San Diego and the beautiful exposition grounds as well.

San Diego Union
GOLDEN FLIER SUFFRAGISTS VISIT FAIR
The suffragists and their cat mascot which plainly showed the effects of the desert trip, were surrounded on the plaza de Panama by hundreds of Exposition visitors and questioned concerning the trip of 4343 miles which has taken them through the principal cities of the east and south. Mrs. Burke said that bad roads were the rule during most of the trip and that in parts of the south they were almost impassable. She declared that the roads encountered in San Diego county were boulevards compared to some they passed over in the south. Owing to the poor condition of the roads, the Golden Flyer is ten days behind schedule.

....When asked her opinion on the jury of women which tried a recent case in this city, Mrs. Burke said "I believe that women should have a place on the jury, as well as men. A jury composed of men and women is only compatible with our beliefs that women should have equal rights with men."

After a tour of the Exposition grounds which they termed "most beautiful" Mrs. Burke and Miss Richardson were entertained in the woman's board headquarters by local suffrage workers. A musical program was given and the visiting suffragists made a few remarks.

Dr. Charlotte Raker presided at the reception yesterday afternoon. It was decided to have a street meeting at Seventh Street and Broadway tonight beginning at 8 o'clock. Mrs Burke and Miss Richardson will speak from their famous golden flyer.

Two days will be spent in the city before the start of the return trip is made which will include San Francisco, Seattle, Minneapolis, Chicago, Detroit, and intermediate points. The Golden Flier contains a large personal wardrobe of suits and evening gowns and carries a duplicate part for every section of the car. The body and fenders are covered with names in pencil of thousands of persons who have been encountered on their transcontinental journey.

Executive secretary H. J. Penfeld presented each of the suffragists with a bronze button awarded for traveling more than 500 miles to the Exposition.[70]

DAY 59 & 60: SATURDAY & SUNDAY, JUNE 3–4, 1916
SAN DIEGO

The Golden Flyer remained on display for a few days at Mr. Smith's Saxon showroom at the corner of First and C. streets. Though the car looked clean and relatively perky, the wear and tear was evident. The dent in the radiator cowl was just a small bruise now lost among the other dings and signatures and no longer called attention to itself.

Coronado Eagle and Journal
Miss Nell Richardson and Mrs. Alice Snitjer Burke, accompanied by Mrs. Burke's father and brother, were Coronado visitors last Saturday lunching at the Coronado Court Apartments' dining room. Mrs. Burke is a great admirer of Col. Roosevelt, and said she "thought he was the grandest man that ever lived, and if he was nominated, she would go out and work for him." The ladies made an auto trip across the continent, advocating votes for women, and advertising a motor car. She said they asked Col. Roosevelt to christen the car when they started, but he declined the honor, as he didn't want to establish a precedent.[71]

DAY 61: MONDAY, JUNE 5, 1916
SAN DIEGO TO LOS ANGELES
APPROXIMATELY 4,415 MILES TRAVELED

Los Angeles Times

Mrs. Alice Snitjer Burke and Miss Nell Richardson, well known women suffrage advocates, who left New York, April 6, in a Saxon automobile on a transcontinental trip, will arrive in this city at noon today. They will be escorted to the City Hall by a delegation of local suffrage workers. The women will be given a welcome to Los Angeles by the Mayor and in the afternoon will attend a meeting of the Women's City Club at Blanchard Hall.[72]

DAY 63: WEDNESDAY, JUNE 7, 1916
LOS ANGELES TO BAKERSFIELD
APPROXIMATELY 4,526 MILES TRAVELED

Los Angeles Times

SPREADING THE GOSPEL OF VOTES FOR WOMEN

After two days of earnest hustling about in their yellow Saxon, euphoniously known as the "Golden Flyer", Miss Nell Richardson and Mrs. Alice Snitjer Burke, transcontinental suffragists, will leave for the north this morning.

The ladies are carrying a tremendous lot of luggage—three evening dresses, fluffy, bouffant creations of many layered tulle, three afternoon gowns, fourteen dresses, ten shirt waists, two tailored suits, two rain coats, two sweaters, a tiny Singer sewing machine, and a small Corona typewriter, besides extra parts for their automobile—extra springs, two axles, two sets of chains, extra tires, transmission and steering gear—everything necessary for a long trip but food. For they aim to always make a hotel by night.

Mrs. Burke is mechanician, and has been at the wheel the entire distance.

Plans have gone awry because of several delays en route, and that is why more club and suffrage women will not have an opportunity of meeting the travelers here, for they must go on to San Jose, home of Mrs. Burke's parents, for a big reception on Friday and to San Francisco, where a big demonstration will send them on their eastward return trip.

The women left the eastern metropolis April 6 and have traveled 4512 miles, coming via Atlanta, across Texas, where they stayed for three weeks, on to Yuma and Los Angeles. They have had bad roads just about everywhere, until reaching Southern California and at one place on the desert something went wrong, and they had to start out to walk after 8 o'clock at night.

Striking out alone on the still, strange desert isn't alluring, even to those more familiar with its mysteries than two young women, whose principal excitement up to a few months ago was waging an active campaign for equal rights and captaining long parades and demonstrations. But they courageously took some water and their little black kitten (they wouldn't part with their mascot for anything short of universal suffrage) and started out. At the end of six and a half miles they found some one to help them.

Miss Nell Richardson also displays a diamond back snake skin with nine rattlers as a trophy of their eventful trip.

They had to wrap Saxon, their cat, in wet cloths coming across the desert, because he is so tiny, and they have had an awful time keeping him alive. Even they are a bit worn out—very brown and blistered—but full of enthusiasm.[73]

DAY 64: THURSDAY, JUNE 8, 1916
BAKERSFIELD TO MODESTO
APPROXIMATELY 4,728 MILES TRAVELED

Modesto Evening News
Mrs. Burke received a pleasant surprise upon reaching Modesto by meeting for the first time in ten years a daughter, Miss Armstrong, who came yesterday from San Jose.[74]

DAY 65: FRIDAY, JUNE 9, 1916
MODESTO TO SAN JOSE
APPROXIMATELY 4,815 MILES TRAVELED

San Jose Mercury News
The Chamber of Commerce has been called on by the women and girls of San Jose to furnish at least 25 automobiles to take them out on the Milpitas Road near the city limits tomorrow (Friday) after-

noon at 3:30 PM, there to meet and escort Mrs. Alice Snitjer Burke into the city and hold a public reception on the courthouse steps.

Mrs. Burke is a native of San Jose and is campaigning in the interest of women's suffrage, having come across the country from Washington, DC, in an automobile. Every city along the route has met her enthusiastically with large delegations of women and girls and given her a public reception. Mayor P. R. Husted, John D. Kuster, P.B. Brown and Joseph T Brooks have been appointed a committee from the Women's organizations to meet Mrs. Burke and the mayor will present her with a large key to San Jose provided by the chamber of commerce.

All persons who can possibly spare a machine to take the local delegation to meet Mrs. Burke are requested by the Chamber of Commerce to meet at the Chamber of Commerce, Market and Santa Clara Streets, Friday afternoon at 3:30 PM fill the machines with the local ladies and girls, go out the Oakland Road beyond the city limits, meet Mrs. Burke and escort her to the court house steps. The entire reception will require not more than an hour, or perhaps one hour and a half at the most.

The school children will line up along the three blocks north of the courthouse and will throw flowers as Mrs. Burke drives by, but School Superintendent Sheriffs ask the mothers to turn out to look after them so they will be perfectly safe.

The key is to be carried across the continent on the shield of the automobile and has inscribed on it "San Jose, California".[75]

DAY 66: SATURDAY, JUNE 10, 1916
SAN JOSE AREA

Alice and Nell planned to spend two weeks in the San Jose area. Though they were taking advantage of downtime to visit friends and family, they did not stop telling their audiences about their travels.

San Jose Mercury
Telling of the thrilling experiences and hardships through which they had passed on their trip by automobile from New York to California, and of the campaign for women's suffrage which has been waged in New York, Alice Snitzer [sic] Burke and her companion Miss Nell

Richardson spoke under the auspices of the Woman's Civic League at the first Baptist Church last evening.

Mrs. Nelly Thompson president of the Civic league presided over the meeting and introduce[ed] Miss Richardson as the first speaker. She told of the campaign which had been waged in New York to get the equal suffrage bill introduced in the assembly and the senate stating that for many weeks 100 Street meetings were held in greater New York each night.

"You have no idea what New York women are up against," said Miss Richardson.

"This city is run by Tammany Hall and the upper state is run by a Republican machine."

She told of the difficulties with which the workers had met and of many of the encouraging things which they had encountered, and spoke in high terms of the courage and determination of the women who were working for their freedom. She told of the work which had been done in the assembly and senate and of how the women waited patiently outside the committee rooms all day, many of them taking their lunches, so that they might be on the ground when action was taken on the bill.

At one mass meeting the committee raised $100,000 with which to carry on the work of the organization and at the suffrage ball held in Madison Square Garden nearly $10,000 was raised. She also told of the suffrage parade in which 35,000 people participated.

At the conclusion of Miss Richardson's address, Mrs. Thompson told of the work which is being done for the establishment of a day nursery where the children of working women may be cared for. She then introduced Alice Snitzer [sic] Burke who told of the trip which she and Miss Richardson had taken across the United States in the interest of women's suffrage.

The speaker told of her first determination to make the trip and of the difficulties which she and Miss Richardson had encountered in getting started. A terrific blizzard was encountered shortly after the start was made and after leaving Washington to get to Fredericksburg, what the speaker termed as "the worst road in America" was encountered. Forced to drive at night without lights stalled in the center of creeks, stuck in the mud and finally obliged to remain by the side of the road all night, the travelers did not lose courage but continued on through the southern states encountering dangers and hardships.

The speaker told of the bad roads through Texas and of the fact that all of the men went armed about the streets. At several of the towns where they remained they were warned that if the fire bell rang they should run for the school house without even waiting to dress, as it would be a signal that the Mexicans were raiding the town. The two women were stalled on the road in the center of a barren waste where the only person is in sight were Mexican horsemen.

More trouble and hardships were in countered in crossing the desert, the two women finally reaching Yuma, Arizona, 11 days behind their schedule.

In closing her address this speaker urged the women here to realize what a help they could be to the women of the east in winning the battle for suffrage. She stated that the suffrage battle would not be won and the country would not be really a free country until there was equal suffrage all over the nation.[76]

DAY 70: WEDNESDAY, JUNE 14, 1916
SAN FRANCISCO
APPROXIMATELY 4,863 MILES TRAVELED

Oakland Tribune
FAMOUS WOMEN MOTORISTS ARRIVE
New York to Coast in Auto for Cause of Suffrage
On Wednesday last, when Mrs. Alice Snitjer Burke reached San Francisco in her husky little Saxon roadster, two months and eight days after she left New York, she completed the half-way mark in her famous journey around the United States in the cause of women suffrage—one of the most remarkable motor-car journeys ever undertaken by a woman.[77]

Riverside Independent Enterprise
One of the best known suffragette leaders, Alice Snitzer Burke, of the Bronx County suffrage league, and her famous little "Yellow Car" will appear in the forthcoming Edison comedy, "A Sport by Circumstance." The film catches her in characteristically energetic

speeches which are events at one hundred and forty-ninth street and third avenue, New York. The comedy features the new Edison comedian, Raymond McKee, and is directed by the new Edison director, Will Louis. McKee appears as a minister, who, through a case of mistaken identity, is made to ride in a highly ludicrous horse race.[78]

JUNE 14–28

Alice and Nell spent two weeks in San Jose visiting family and resting in San Jose, California.

DAY 84: WEDNESDAY, JUNE 28, 1916
SAN JOSE–SAN FRANCISCO–BERKELEY–SACRAMENTO
APPROXIMATELY 5,265 MILES TRAVELED

Oakland Tribune
SUFFRAGISTS FLIT IN AND THEN FLIT OUT OF BERKELEY.
FLYING SQUADRON HAS THREE MEMBERS—ONE IS A KITTEN.
The flying squadron of suffrage, with its three members, Mrs. Alice Snitzer Burke, Miss Nell Richardson and a tiny black kitten for a mascot, got into Berkeley and out again with flying colors. Pausing here for luncheon, which the representatives of the feminist cause had nearly forgotten in the excitement of their departure, they were again northbound before sundown.

Mrs. Mary McHenry Keith, whose husband was William Keith, the internationally famed painter, and who has been for years one of the State's suffrage leaders, entertained the automobilists at her home at Ridge Road and Le Roy Avenue for two hours in the afternoon. They were accompanied to Mrs. Keith's by Mrs. Mary Harding Gammage, president of the local counsel [sic] and other members of the suffrage force on both sides of the bay.

In San Francisco, Mrs. Burke and Miss Richardson were welcome to by Mayor James Rolph Jr. They were accompanied to the ferry by a large party of friends and well-wishers and bidden God-speed on their return journey. Judge William J. Muraskey made the chief speech of farewell.

They left Berkeley for Sacramento, and will do the Northwest on their return.[79]

DAY 87: SATURDAY, JULY 1, 1916
CAMP JOHNSON
(OUTSIDE SACRAMENTO AT THE FAIR GROUNDS).

SUFFRAGETTES INVADE CAMP OF GUARDSMEN

Camp Johnson had what might be called a "visitation" or an "invasion" to-day. Two suffragettes, all the way from New York, appeared in camp, with a pennant-belecked [sic] auto carrying the suffragette slogan: "Votes for Woman."

They visited the Los Angeles troops and immediately were surrounded by several hundred curious soldiers bent on seeing what a real live suffragette looks like. Then they went to the Fifth Regiment camp and the boys from the Bay Region made things lively by keeping the two women busy seeing that the soldiers did not walk away with the little runabout.

Post cards were distributed, the women answered hundreds of questions, and the soldiers wrote their names all over the car, which is a yellow-enameled finish.

The speedometer registered 5,265 miles this morning. As the yellow car carrying the two suffragettes chugged from the camp the soldiers gave them a lusty cheer.[80]

It was time for the ladies to drive north.

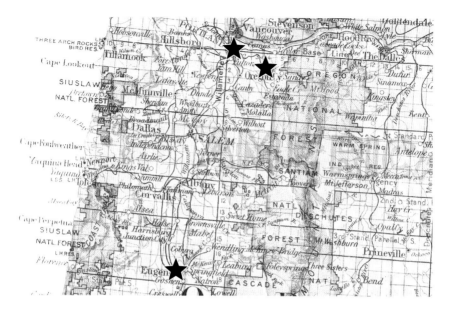

OREGON

DAY 92: THURSDAY, JULY 6, 1916
EUGENE, OR
APPROXIMATELY 5,744 MILES TRAVELED

Morning Register (Eugene, OR)

"Conditions near Mexico are really frightful," said Mrs Burk last night. "The people are in a continual state of terror. The Mexicans make their raids at night across the border, commit their depredations, carry off the women and divide them up among the men after getting back across to safety."

"Every person we saw was armed, either carrying a rifle or a large revolver, and we were certainly glad to get out of that country. We spent three weeks in Texas."

Mrs. Burke believes that the Sacramento canyon road is the most dangerous one she has encountered an [sic] the trip; and the lack of road signs that give adequate and reliable information and the conditions of roads caused her to speak in no uncertain tones of some of the Pacific coast highways.

We have had a most exciting trip and have encountered many obstacles. The roads in this part of the country, though not so bad north of the California line, are most disappointing.

"I have a notion to become a good roads enthusiast and take another trip after I have returned from this one," said Mrs. Burke last night.

Owing to the existence of suffrage in Oregon their stay is not so long here; but they are killing time, for they are not due in Portland until July 17. From Portland they will go to Seattle.

Practically the only trouble they have had is a few punctures, going the first 4600 miles without even tire trouble. The two front tires have not yet sustained a puncture. No engine trouble has been encountered, they state.[81]

DAY 94: SATURDAY, JULY 8, 1916
EUGENE TO PORTLAND, OR
APPROXIMATELY 5,854 MILES TRAVELED

Oregonian (Portland, OR)
HOPE LIES IN WEST
STAR OF SUFFRAGE LOOMS BEYOND ROCKIES, SAYS WORKER—HAZARDOUS TRAIL TAKEN—NEW YORK WOMEN'S SCORN IN PRESENCE OF MAN ON AUTO TRIP ACROSS CONTINENT IN CAMPAIGN TO HELP EXTEND BALLOT TO THEIR SISTERS

"The fate of national suffrage rests with the women of the West," says Mrs. Alice Snitger Burke, of New York. That is one reason why she and her co-worker, Miss Nell Richardson, also of New York, came dashing into Portland early yesterday morning in a saucy little chrome yellow motorcar, bedecked with the "keys" of the various cities they have visited and "Votes for Women" banners.

Mrs. Burke and Miss Richardson have made a hazardous auto trip from New York City through the South and California to Portland to spread the doctrine of suffrage. They are heart and soul in the work and have had a risky but eventful trip in which they have traveled through every border state in America. They will return by auto and will cover 57 [sic] states before the trip is ended.

SOUTH NOT LOST TO CAUSE
"The idea that the South is bitter against suffrage is all wrong," said Mrs. Burke. "The Southern men will give their women the ballot at anytime they want it."

"In the East," says Mrs. Burke, "it's harder. We have labor conditions, politics and corruption to contend with. Yes, the Eastern women must look to the West. There rests the hope of National Suffrage."

Although Miss Richardson is also a suffrage speaker, she confines her opinions to the platform and bubbles about the trip. She laughs over the times that they have lain under the car on the hot desert sands of Texas and New Mexico and adjusted bolts and screws. No, indeed: she didn't see any need of a man along to spoil the trip.

To look at the gay little car that has made the trip, no one would suppose there was much in it besides the two suffrage workers. But the truth is that when they begin their trip they stacked in everything they might need. A tiny sewing machine, a typewriter, electric iron, kodak, evening gowns, ten shirtwaists, four dinner and afternoon dresses, lingerie, stockings, sweaters, blankets and lots of other things are carried.

To the four winds goes the superstition that a black cat is a hoodoo." "Their's isn't. For a jet-black cat, Saxon, their mascot, has ridden from New York to Portland on top of the seat.

Sometimes when their car had sunk to hubs in the sand in the deserts they walked to a nearby town for assistance, but they have put on tires and fixed their car over and over again.

"Once in New Mexico," said Miss Richardson, "we were stuck—just couldn't move. It was 8 o'clock and night was falling. We took the revolver, our water bag and the cat and walked five miles to town.

I HAVE A NOTION TO BECOME A GOOD ROADS
ENTHUSIAST AND TAKE ANOTHER TRIP
AFTER I HAVE RETURNED FROM THIS ONE,"
SAID MRS. BURKE.

That was only one of their experiences, but they are happy over them. They will remain in Portland until Tuesday morning and then go to Seattle and East by way of Montana. A rather extensive campaign of South Dakota will be made: then they will go East to New York again.

The suffrage work is quite new to Miss Richardson, but Mrs. Burke has been at it for the past six years. For 165 consecutive days she spoke every night in New York City from eight until 12, later touring the state. Both Miss Richardson and Mrs. Burke say that the doctrine of "votes for women" is winning favor everywhere.

"Both men and women have ceased to regard it as 'new-fangled' and most of them regard it as necessary, says Mrs. Burke. "If only some of you Western women would go back and speak and show some of the Eastern men the suffragettes are not monstrosities, the cause would progress faster."[82]

DAY 96: MONDAY, JULY 10, 1916
PORTLAND, OR

Oregon Daily Journal

The women arrived in Portland Saturday noon and had prepared to leave Monday morning. But they were delayed two days by having the machine overhauled.

The stay in Portland was quite a rest for the suffragists. Previous to their arrival here they had been giving from one to five speeches a day and were compelled to enter into all sorts of festivities in their honor.

But, with the exception of conferences and discussions with woman club workers and a few entertainments, the travelers have enjoyed a three days' rest.

Dr. Esther Pohl-Lovejoy gave a dinner at the Hotel Portland for the suffrage workers last night at which many prominent suffragists were present.

Mrs Burke and Miss Richardson will spend a few days in both Tacoma and Seattle, after which they will start on the last leg of their journey.[83]

DAY 97: TUESDAY, JULY 11, 1916
PORTLAND, OR

Oregonian
VOTES ARE PLEDGED.
TOURING SUFFRAGISTS WIN MANY PROMISES OF SUPPORT.
HIGHWAY TRIP IS ENJOYED MRS. BURKE AND MISS
RICHARDSON AND THEIR BLACK KITTEN DRIVE OVER
SCENIC BOULEVARD AND HEAR PLAUDITS OF CROWD.

"Of all the scenery that we have seen from New York, through the South and to Oregon, nothing has been so wonderful as the Columbia River Highway," said Mrs. Alice Snitger Burke, when she arrived in Portland after she and her fellow worker, Miss Nell Richardson, had passed Sunday on the highway.

"Persons stopped us everywhere, and we had a wonderful time," said Miss Richardson. Both waxed warm in their praise of Oregon and the people and Portland.

"We've got six votes for you," yelled a motorist on the highway.

"Any girl that can handle a car like that could have me and my votes," chimed another.

"Where is the cat?" called many.

The black kitten was there. He sat on the seat as primly as you please, and wasn't a bit afraid of the crowds. That's the way he has taken the whole trip.

Arriving in Portland about 6 o'clock the suffragists took dinner at a downtown restaurant. Crowds flocked about the curious little yellow car, and did not leave until the owners came out to take their machine away. "Votes for Women" banner, and a great key, from the mayor of San Jose presented them, adorn the machine. Many of the bystanders became bold enough to write or scratch their names on the body of the car, which is already well decked with signatures.

Passersby on the Columbia River Highway yesterday asked Mrs. Burke and Mrs. [sic] Richardson about their expected trip to Seattle, and advise them to abandon the idea, saying that there were many places flooded so that a car cannot pass. If that is true the suffragists will ship their car to Seattle tomorrow morning, and if not they will motor to Seattle, leaving early tomorrow.[84]

DAY 98: WEDNESDAY, JULY 12, 1916
PORTLAND TO KELSO, OR
APPROXIMATELY 5,903 MILES TRAVELED

The car is shipped north to Kelso due to flooding and bad roads.

Oregonian
SUFFRAGISTS ARE TO LEAVE TODAY.
MRS. BURKE AND MRS. [SIC] RICHARDSON TO CONTINUE
COAST-TO-COAST TOUR IN AUTO. VISITORS ARE
MUCH FETED. CONFERENCE IS HELD WITH PORTLAND
CLUBWOMEN—HARD CAMPAIGN TO BE WAGED IN
SOUTH DAKOTA EN ROUTE TO NEW YORK.

Mrs. Alice Snitger Burke and Miss Nell Richardson, New York suffragists, who Saturday reached Portland on their transcontinental round-trip tour in a midget automobile, will leave Portland for Seattle this morning. The tiny automobile, which has been viewed by hundreds since it's unpretentious arrival in the city, will be shipped to Kelso, owing to a bad stretch of road between Portland and Kelso, but from there the trip will continue by road.

The object of the trip is to create a new interest in suffrage for women, and while they have no active work to do in Oregon, they have been busy while here, with entertainment and discussion with some of the front-rank women's club workers and suffragists.

Dr. Esther Pohl Lovejoy entertained the traveling suffragists at dinner at Hotel Portland last night. Mrs. Frederick Eggert and Mrs. Sarah A. Evans were among the guests.

Mrs. Burke and Miss Richardson will spend a few days in Seattle and Tacoma and take the Northern route back to New York. They are going prepared to wage a hard campaign in South Dakota. They expect to reach New York in August. The black cat, which due to some cause unknown to the suffragists, is turning white, will be taken all the way back. The cat enjoys the riding, the women say.[85]

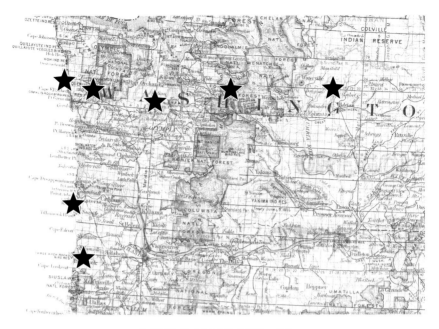

WASHINGToN

DAY 99: THURSDAY, JULY 13, 1916
KELSO TO SEATTLE, WA
APPROXIMATELY 6,029 MILES TRAVELED

Seattle Star

LOCAL "SUFFS" AWAIT LITTLE YELLOW AUTO

Seattle suffragists are on the lookout for a yellow automobile bearing Miss Nell Richardson and Mrs. Alice S. Burke, Eastern suffragists, due to arrive Thursday from Portland with a message on women's rights.

Miss Adella Parker said the Seattle women in all probability will entertain the visitors, especially if they aren't anti-Wilson advocates.[86]

Seattle Star

"SUFFS" TO SPEAK SATURDAY TO CLUB

After completing their coast-to-coast suffrage swing, Miss Nell Richardson and Mrs. Alice Burke of New York are acquainting themselves with Seattle Friday, preparatory to their talk on women's rights Saturday noon, before the King County Democratic Club.[87]

DAY 102–105: JULY 16, 17, 18, 19
SEATTLE, WASHINGTON–NORTH BEND–ROSLYN–
WENATCHEE–SNOHOMISH PASS

Even though it was July, the Golden Flyer and its occupants became bogged down in snow just east of Seattle in Snoqualmie Pass and needed extra days to complete the passage.

Spokane Chronicle
LOOK FOR SUFFRAGE AUTO.
Women interested in suffrage are waiting anxiously to hear from the "Golden Flyer," a little automobile in which Mrs. Burke and Miss Richardson are traveling across the country. The names of the two members of the party had been forwarded to Miss Reba J Hurn in Spokane by Rhea M. Whitehead of Seattle, the woman justice of the peace.

"They are supposed to be on their way to Spokane," Miss Hurn said today, "and they want a chance to speak before some gatherings. They represent the national suffrage association of which Mrs. Carey Chapman Catt is president, and have toured across the United States and their machine. I hope they haven't met with trouble on Washington state roads."[88]

DAY 107: FRIDAY, JULY 21
SPOKANE, WA
APPROXIMATELY 6,345 MILES TRAVELED

DAY 108: SATURDAY, JULY 22
SPOKANE, WA

Spokesman-Review (Spokane)
WOMEN ON TOUR OF US IN AUTO
TWO SUFFRAGISTS REACH SPOKANE AFTER PILOTING CAR FROM NEW YORK TO PACIFIC. HOMEWARD BOUND NOW HAVE VISITED ATLANTA, MOBILE, MEXICAN BORDER, SAN DIEGO AND SEATTLE. Claiming to be the first women across the continent alone in an automobile, piloting their car into the four corners of the United

States, Mrs. Alice Snitjer Burke of New York, and Miss Nell Richardson of Winchester, Va., suffrage leaders, aboard their yellow Saxon car, "The Golden Flyer," arrived in Spokane yesterday, and are at the Davenport.

Mrs. Burke, who does the driving, says they have had no trouble except an occasional puncture, and one tire has come all the way from New York and has yet to receive its first puncture. Another was punctured for the first time just before entering Spokane yesterday....

They do no camping, making their jumps so as to reach a hotel for each stop, but they carry two trunks, enameled yellow to match the car, a typewriter and a small sewing machine, and put in their time sewing when not speaking or putting out suffrage literature....

They talked before the Democratic Club at Seattle, have no speaking itinerary in Washington or Idaho, but will resume their suffrage campaign in Montana. They will be at the hotel between 10 and 12 today to meet all interested in the suffrage campaign. While at Wenatchee they registered for Colville lands.

SUFFRAGE STATES NOT EXCITING.

Miss Richardson says it is a lot more exciting to campaign in states where the suffrage has not been granted to women. All their work in such states is by street speaking, but in suffrage states the subject does not seem to hold the interest it does elsewhere. She and Mrs. Burke strongly urge women of suffrage states to help other women get the franchise.

A third member of the party is a tiny black kitten, "Saxon," who rides most of the time on the back of the seat, and has come all the way from New York with the women. They expect to leave this afternoon for Wallace, and plan to reach New York late in September.[89]

IDAHO & MONTANA

DAY 109: SUNDAY, JULY 23
SPOKANE, WA TO WALLACE, ID
APPROXIMATELY 6,345 MILES TRAVELED

DAY 110: MONDAY, JULY 24
WALLACE, ID TO SALTESE, MT AND
CONTINUED EAST ALONG THE YELLOWSTONE TRAIL

Detroit Times

We came through Montana...which will submit the question of prohibition to the voters this fall. All the men from the humblest up, seemed to be eager that the states should be made dry. Many of the liquor men in Montana have closed out their business and are trying to enter new fields. If ever prohibition was needed it is in Montana. In the little town of Saltese, thru which we passed every other man was drunk and other sorts of vice were flourishing.[90]

Detroit Times

In Montana the women are working on a bill to care for the illegitimate child. It will, in effect, mean that there will be no more illegitimate children, but, rather, illegitimate fathers. At present there are six states where a father can will away his children and only 14 where mothers and fathers are equal guardians.[91]

DAY 113: THURSDAY, JULY 27, 1916
ST. REGIS–SUPERIOR–MISSOULA, MT
APPROXIMATELY 6,685 MILES TRAVELED

Missoulian

LADY SUFFRAGISTS MAKE MISSOULA ON TOUR
TWO WOMEN MAKE TRANSCONTINENTAL JAUNT TO EDUCATE MEN ON BALLOT.

Embullient with energetic enthusiasm for woman suffrage and a Saxon runabout, Mrs. Alice Sutjer Burke and Nell Richardson, traveling in the "Saxon Golden Flyer," arrived in Missoula last night on a continental tour, campaigning nationally for votes for women. The two women are representing the National Woman Suffrage association. They left New York city April 6 and are on their way home after a trip including in its itinerary Georgia, Louisiana, the Texas desert, California and Pacific coast points and western Montana.

"I believe prohibition will come before woman suffrage," said Mrs. Burke, who is exceptionally interested in politics, "and I think that it will be several years before women are given the national privilege of voting. Men have to be educated to know the advantages of allowing votes for the female sex and that training to be thorough will likely require more years than we expect."

These two women political tourists have been received loyally wherever they have gone. In San Jose, Cal., the key of the city was turned over to them and they are carrying it home as a souvenir of the occasion. It was made of wood. When they left New York, bands played for them and, according to Mrs. Burke's description, hundreds of cameramen snapped them and their car. Many moving picture companies are already showing the pictures on the screen.

The transcontinental trip Mrs. Burke and Nell Richardson are making is possibly the only one of its kind ever attempted, and they deserve credit for the skill they have shown in driving a Saxon car across the continent. The car, a four-cylinder runabout, is painted yellow and is decorated with suffrage pennants and characteristic insignias. The little Saxon car was examined at the McCullough Motor Car garage last night and found to have withstood the strain of thousands of miles on the worst roads in the United States admirably. The drivers said that they repeatedly climbed hill after hill which could not be negotiated by larger machines.

Mrs. Burke is a strong prohibitionist and said that she may make another transcontinental trip next year in favor of the movement.

The two women carried as a companion a small kitten, which is claim to be the only one to have survived a continental jaunt. Mrs. Burke said that the feline spent its time along the road chasing rabbits and birds for exercise.

Miss Richardson, who is the road expert of the party, was not favorably impressed with the roads of western Montana and describe them to be very rough, full of dangerous chuch holes and steep in places.[92]

DAY 115: SATURDAY, JULY 29, 1916
DRUMMOND TO ANACONDA, MT
APPROXIMATELY 6,790 MILES TRAVELED

DAY 116: SUNDAY, JULY 30, 1916
ANACONDA TO BUTTE, MT
APPROXIMATELY 6,814 MILES TRAVELED

Anaconda Standard

"When I get through with this trip" declared Miss Burke, driver and guide for the little party, "I am going to take up the fight for good roads. It is a shame that this great and rich nation maintains such frightful roads and I will be able to speak from some very intimate knowledge and sad experience."

"We found little patches of good roads here and there," said Miss Richardson, "and the best piece of road on the whole trip so far is between Drummond and Butte. Many big machines couldn't go where we went and had to turn back, especially north of San Francisco. Rains, floods and washouts have made portions of the roads almost impassable."[93]

DAY 117: MONDAY, JULY 31, 1916
BUTTE, MT
APPROXIMATELY 6,814 MILES TRAVELED

The Butte Miner

Arrived in Butte last night after having traveled more than 7000 miles without the assistance of a man.

While in Butte the visitors probably will not make any formal talks and they may not be able to meet the women of the city at any formal gathering. They will meet in an informal manner as many of the prominent women of the city as it is possible for them to do in the short time they will be in the city.

"The women of Montana and the west must not forget us. They must remember that they themselves are limited in their suffrage just as long as there are states in the nation which do not grant suffrage. If they move from Montana into a state which does not grant suffrage they lose the right to vote."[94]

DAY 118: TUESDAY, AUGUST 1, 1916
BUTTE HEADING EAST TOWARD NORTH DAKOTA

As the ladies mentioned the road conditions along the Yellowstone Trail during their talk in Detroit, we can assume that is the route they took going east.

Anaconda Standard

She...had some harrowing experiences after leaving Butte and declared that $10,000 in advance would be no inducement to make the trip again.[95]

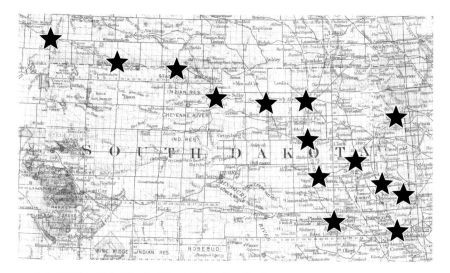

NORTH DAKOTA & SOUTH DAKOTA

DAY 132: TUESDAY, AUGUST 15, 1916
REDFIELD, ND
APPROXIMATELY 7,631 MILES TRAVELED

Aberdeen American

LITTLE "YELLOW CAR" AT REDFIELD

SUFFRAGETTES AT REDFIELD RETURNING
FROM TRANS-CONTINENTAL TOUR.

Redfield has been invaded by the all-conquering forces of the suffragettes and apparently the city is theirs. On Tuesday evening the "Little Yellow Car" driven by Mrs. Burke and Miss Nell Richardson of New York arrived at Redfield on the way back to New York on their trans-continental tour.

The ladies addressed a large crowd on Main Street that evening and blazed the way for the mass attack of yesterday by Mrs. Emma Smith DeVoe of Washington, Mrs. Elsie V. Benedict of Denver and Dr. Effie McCollum Jones of Waterloo, Iowa. Meetings were held in the afternoon at the Commercial hall, and in the evening the ladies spoke to another large audience on the street.

The speakers presented their cause in a clear and forceful manner, and seem to make a good impression. Redfield has a strong local organization and the yellow "Votes for Women" badges were in evidence very largely, and local workers are now claiming a number of converts to their cause as a result of the two days' campaign.

It is the plan of the county organization to send speakers to the various towns in the county from now on and line up Spink county in good shape for the fall election on this question.[96]

DAY 133: WEDNESDAY, AUGUST 16, 1916
REDFIELD TO HURON, SD
APPROXIMATELY 7,980 MILES TRAVELED

The pair arrived in the morning, and delivered an 8:00 P.M. address on Dakota Avenue just east of the First National Bank [97]

DAY 136: SATURDAY, AUGUST 19, 1916
HURON TO WOLSEY TO FARMHOUSE 11 MILES WEST OF HURON

Huron Daily Huronite
YELLOW CAR CAUGHT IN THE RAIN
SUFFRAGE TRAVELERS HAD TO SPEND
SATURDAY NIGHT IN THE COUNTRY.

Mrs. Alice S. Burke and Miss Nell Richardson, the two suffrage workers traveling in the "golden flyer", who have been making their headquarters in this city for several days were caught in the rain Saturday night about eleven miles west of Huron and had to remain overnight at a farm house. The ladies state, however, that their delay in reaching Huron proved a big help for suffrage as they succeeded in converting the farmer's wife at the home where they stayed and the hired man to the cause of suffrage, the farmer, himself, they state, having already taken a stand in favor of "women's rights."

Mrs. Burke and Miss Richardson were returning from Wolsey where they delivered several rousing suffrage speeches before the citizens of that place earlier in the evening Saturday.[98]

DAY 138: MONDAY, AUGUST 21, 1916
HURON
APPROXIMATELY 8,017 MILES TRAVELED

Huron Daily Huronite
The two workers expected to leave Huron today for a campaign in Mitchell and the country near there, but the bad condition of the roads made it impossible for them to make the journey.[99]

DAY 139: TUESDAY, AUGUST 22, 1916
HURON TO MITCHELL
APPROXIMATELY 8,069 MILES TRAVELED

Mitchell Capital (Mitchell, SD)
The speakers on the "Golden Flyer" were mired in the mud near Huron and were unable to get here yesterday [Monday]. They phoned that they had started today and expected to reach the city in time for the meeting tonight.[100]

DAY 140: WEDNESDAY, AUGUST 23, 1916
MITCHELL TO SIOUX FALLS
APPROXIMATELY 8,142 MILES TRAVELED

Argus-Leader (Sioux Falls, SD)
It is reported that a "Golden Flier" car driven by two suffragists,... will reach here this evening. The women have been addressing street meetings along the route which takes them to San Francisco. Dell Rapids expects a visit from the flier tomorrow.[101]

DAY 142: FRIDAY, AUGUST 25, 1916
DELL RAPIDS TO SIOUX FALLS, SD
APPROXIMATELY 8,084 MILES TRAVELED

Letter to the *Argus-Leader*

Sioux Falls, S.D., Aug 25th, 1916
The Power City Auto Company,
Sioux Falls, S. D.

Gentlemen:—You ask what I think of the Saxon car? Well, you couldn't convince me there was a better car on the market than the Saxon. It is easy to operate, manipulate and repair.

We left New York city about four months ago, and have traveled to date 8,500 miles. In all that distance we have had no tire or motor trouble, and have not had the car overhauled. She has traveled over all kinds of roads, up all kinds of hills and mountains, over deserts, and as yet we have never had to "call for help." Some record you'll say. Well in Portland, we were told, it was the first time any car had ever made such a wonderful record and in the hands of two women too. We never have gotten less than 30 miles on the gallon of gas and the greatest mileage we secured was 40 to the gallon. In New York there was not a man, in automobile row, who would say the car would make the loop, but there never was a failure attached to my name, and a little Saxon is going back home.

I wish more women would use the little Saxon, for I know of no better car in the market, and a big tall man will fit in the small Saxon roadster better than any other car, and his knees will not be up under his chin, like most of the modern cars, and he will find real comfort.

Thanking you personally for your courtesy to me while under your care in Sioux Falls, believe me,

Sincerely,
Alice Snitjer Burke,
Pilot of the Golden Flyer[102]

DAY 145: MONDAY, AUGUST 28, 1916
SIOUX FALLS TO FLANDREU

DAY 146: TUESDAY, AUGUST 29, 1916
FLANDREU TO BROOKINGS

DAY 147: WEDNESDAY, AUGUST 30, 1916
BROOKINGS AREA TO BRYANT[103]
APPROXIMATELY 8,509 MILES TRAVELED

DAY 148: THURSDAY, AUGUST 31, 1916
BRYANT TO MILBANK, SD[104]
APPROXIMATELY 8,592 MILES TRAVELED

Why South Dakota Was So Important

Alice and Nell had planned on spending two weeks in South Dakota as the state had a referendum on suffrage coming up for a vote in November. The suffrage movement in South Dakota had been gaining momentum for several years, with suffragists advocating for equal voting rights but now it was time to really push the vote.

The South Dakota suffrage referendum took place on November 7, 1916. The question put to the voters was whether the South Dakota constitution should be amended to grant women the right to vote in the state. The amendment read:

"Shall Article VII of the constitution of the State of South Dakota be amended by adding a new section thereto, to be known as Section 22, which said Section 22 shall provide that the right to vote at all elections shall not be denied or abridged on account of sex, and that women may participate in all elections upon the same terms as men?"

Of the 111,582 votes cast, 58,350 votes (52.2%) of the voting population said no. Only 47.8% said yes. Though close, it was not a win for suffrage. It took until November 5, 1918, for South Dakota to grant women the right to vote.

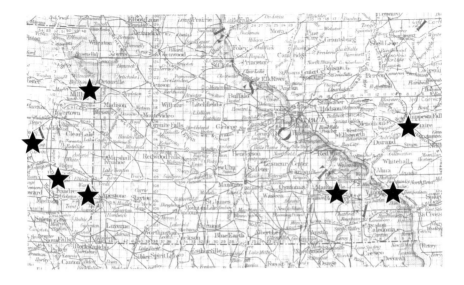

MINNESoTA

DAY 149: FRIDAY, SEPTEMBER 1, 1916
MILBANK TO OLIVIA, MN
APPROXIMATELY 8,696 MILES TRAVELED

DAY 150: SATURDAY, SEPTEMBER 2, 1916
OLIVIA TO MINNEAPOLIS[105]
APPROXIMATELY 8,793 MILES TRAVELED

DAY 152: MONDAY, SEPTEMBER 4, 1916
MINNEAPOLIS

The Minneapolis Political Equality club will occupy the suffrage booth at the State Fair all day today and will have a table in the Hall of Fame....Mrs. Alice Burke and Miss Nell Richardson of New York, the women who have motored 5,000 miles from coast to coast in the cause of suffrage, will speak at the political equality booth, and will be at the fair from 11 o'clock this morning until evening.[106]

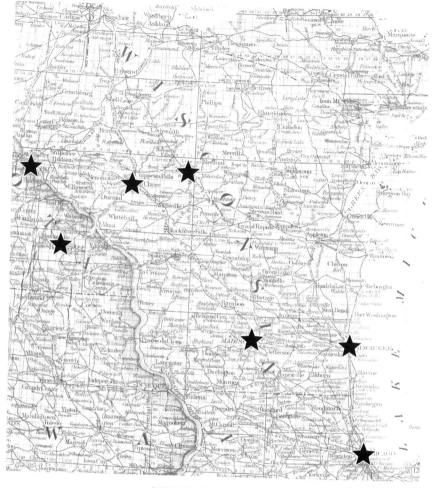

WIS©NSIN

La Crosse Tribune

GOTHAM SUFFRAGE ADVOCATES
MAKE CITY ON JOURNEY

Arriving over the National Park highway in one of the smallest cars which ever arrived in La Crosse, and bearing "votes for women" tags and banners, Miss Nellie Richardson and Mrs. Alice I. Burke spent Friday night in La Crosse.

The women are representatives of the national organization of women suffragists and are touring in their diminutive auto from New York city to San Francisco.

They were to have made addresses here, but were held up on the road by tire trouble and did not arrive until late in the evening.

They scattered a quantity of "votes for women" tags around the Hotel Stoddard lobby and resumed their journey early Saturday morning.[107]

DAY 158: SUNDAY, SEPTEMBER 10, 1916
LA CROSSE TO MADISON, WI
APPROXIMATELY 9,112 MILES TRAVELED

DAY 159: MONDAY, SEPTEMBER 11, 1916
MADISON TO MILWAUKEE
APPROXIMATELY 9,190 MILES TRAVELED

Wisconsin State Journal

"We haven't had any tire trouble or engine or trouble of any sort," said Mrs. Burke as she directed the tightening of bolts on her car in the Jacobson and Austin garage.

"We've been met by parades and demonstrations wherever we went, and the newspapers have given us front page articles with pictures.

"No, I can't say whether I favor Wilson or Hughs for the presidency. The National association is non-partisan."

The suffragists are traveling in the Saxon car of the most brilliant yellow with their itinerary lettered on the doorway: New York, New Orleans, Los Angeles, San Francisco, Seattle, Minneapolis, Chicago, Detroit, New York. Signatures, names of towns and greetings our scrawled over the body of the car, and a yellow suffrage banner is furied aloft as a standard.

"This is the longest tour ever made by automobile," said Mrs. Burke. "At least we can't find a record of any car having made a longer one.

"We are carrying lots of baggage—five afternoon dresses, two evening gowns, twenty shirtwaists, raincoats, sweaters, suits, hats." Thus dispelling the impression that a suffragist and a motoring suffragist at that, is not interested in the feminine accomplishment of being well-dressed.

Mrs. Burke expressed regret that her telegrams to Madison suffragists had evidently miscarried as there was no meeting, demonstration or other recognition of the staunch little car and its mission.[108]

Hotel Stoddard *Wisconsin Historical Society*

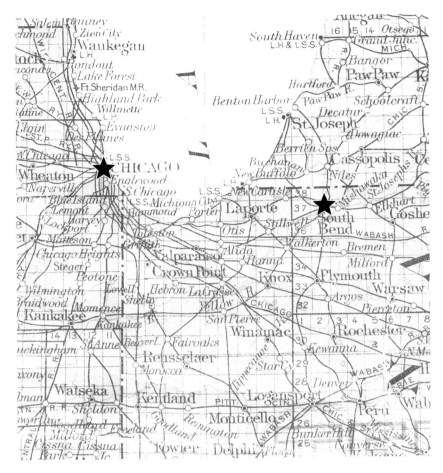

ILLINOIS & INDIANA

Chicago Tribune

En route by automobile from the Pacific to the Atlantic Coast, Miss Nell Richardson, and Mrs. Alice Burke reached Chicago last night from Milwaukee and stopped at the headquarters of the Illinois Equal Suffrage association in the Tower building. The two women completed the transcontinental trip westward some time ago, and then decided to return as they had gone. The jaunt is to advertise "the cause".[109]

DAY 161: WEDNESDAY, SEPTEMBER 13, 1916
CHICAGO TO SOUTH BEND, IN
APPROXIMATELY 9,376 MILES TRAVELED

South Bend News-Times
COVERING NATION IN SAXON WORKING FOR SUFFRAGE FOR WOMEN

Alice Snitjer Burke and Nell Richardson of New York paused in South Bend over night one day this week and then continued their trip on east.

The young women are making the auto trip through 25 states under the direction and as members of the National Suffrage association making rigorous speeches and appeals to large audiences in every city where they have stopped. They were granted the free use of a Saxon car by the Saxon Co. to enable the manufacturers to demonstrate the road endurance contained in one of these small automobiles.

The Saxon car was quartered at the Franklin Motor Car Co.[110]

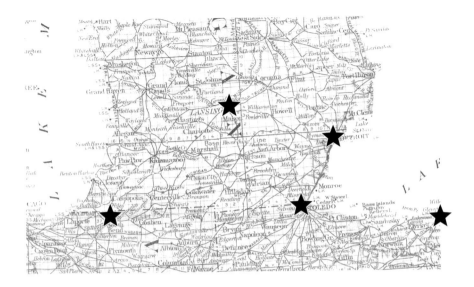

MICHIGAN & OHIO

Grand Rapids Press
SUFFRAGISTS TRAVEL 6500 MILES IN AUTO

DETROIT, SEPT 15—A small yellow automobile carr[y]ing two women arrived here today. It has traveled 6,500 miles from New York to San Francisco and is now on its way back again. Its occupants are Mrs. Alice S. Burke and Miss Nell Richardson, New York suffrage workers, who are also the first women to make a tour of the United States by automobile.[111]

Detroit Free Press
MRS. BURKE WON'T TALK ON POLITICS

ARDENT SUFFRAGIST ARRIVES IN DETROIT. KEEN FOR WOMAN'S RIGHTS, BUT NAUGHT ELSE.

Compared with her ardor when the subject of roads was discussed, Mrs. Alice Snitzer Burke, New York suffragist who is visiting Detroit in the course of a 6,500-mile automobile tour of the United States in a tiny yellow car named the "Golden Flier," maintains unvarying calm when political issues are mentioned. With the exception, naturally, of suffrage, which she declares has been her inspiration through the long days of the trip.

"Roads," said Mrs. Burke emphatically, her eyes snapping, "roads! Nobody on earth can describe the roads of the United States. They are a disgrace to the country. Yellowstone Trail and Pacific Highway are beautiful titles, but the roads they are given to are terrible."

Mrs. Burke spoke at a street meeting in front of the county building Saturday night.[112]

DAY 168: WEDNESDAY, SEPTEMBER 20, 1916
TOLEDO, OH TO CLEVELAND
APPROXIMATELY 9,819 MILES TRAVELED

Why Warren, Pennsylvania?

Warren, Pennsylvania, situated in the northwestern part of the state, has deep ties to the oil industry, stemming back to the mid-ninteenth century.

The US oil boom began in 1859 when Edwin L. Drake successfully drilled the first commercial oil well near Titusville, a town close to Warren. This discovery transformed the region, including Warren, into a bustling center for the nascent oil industry.

Warren's location along the Allegheny River made it a crucial point for transporting oil. The river facilitated the movement of crude oil to refineries, and the town soon became enveloped in the growing industry with refineries, storage facilities, and related businesses sprouting up. The oil wealth resulted in grand mansions and buildings from that era.

Apart from its rich oil history, Warren is also known for its natural beauty, being a gateway to the Allegheny National Forest. Perhaps Alice and Nell thought the detour would be interesting.

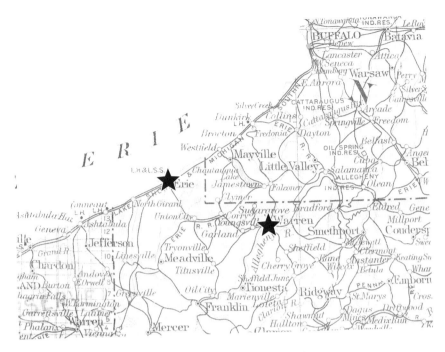

PENNSYLVANIA

DAY 169: THURSDAY, SEPTEMBER 21, 1916

CLEVELAND TO ERIE, PA

APPROXIMATELY 9,921 MILES TRAVELED

DAY 170: FRIDAY, SEPTEMBER 22, 1916

ERIE, PA TO WARREN, PA

APPROXIMATELY 9,987 MILES TRAVELED

NEW YORK

DAY 171: SATURDAY, SEPTEMBER 23, 1916
WARREN, PA TO BUFFALO, NY
APPROXIMATELY 10,082 MILES TRAVELED

Buffalo Morning Express and Illustrated Express
The suffragists will all be out on Buffalo streets today looking for a small yellow automobile....

So successful was Mrs. Burke's trip then [in 1915] that the long coast to coast drive was decided upon....They carried not only their luggage and Mrs. Burke's celebrated crocheting, with which she occupied her spare moments on her last trip, but a complete repair kit and cooking outfit.

...When they reached Dallas on May 11th the troops were mobilizing and the border raids had begun. At Alpine, Tex., where a raid was expected, they were "frankly scared to death," but still game to go on. From there on they ran along border states and had many adventures. By June they were running up the Pacific coast and on July 1st had reached their turning point in Oregon and were headed due east for the home run.

...She will reach Rochester tomorrow, Syracuse on the 25th, Utica on the 26th, Albany on the 27th, and Poughkeepsie on the 28th... will speak at a street meeting on Church near Main Street under the auspices of the Buffalo headquarters, No. 121 Franklin St.[113]

OF ALL THE ABOMINABLE THINGS THAT YOU MET ON THE ROAD, [BRILLIANT HEADLIGHTS] ARE THE WORST

DAY 172: SUNDAY, SEPTEMBER 24, 1916
BUFFALO TO ROCHESTER, NY
APPROXIMATELY 10,158 MILES TRAVELED

Democrat and Chronicle
NEVER TOO BADLY BUMPED TO
TALK EQUAL SUFFRAGE
WOMEN IN GOLDEN FLYER ARRIVE IN ROCHESTER. HAVE
RIDDEN 10,000 MILES— MRS. ALICE S BURKE, AFTER DRIVING
CAR THROUGH WEST AND SOUTH, SAYS SHE IS THINKING
OF TAKING STUMP FOR GOOD ROADS—CAT ESCORT

The Golden Flier, carrying Mrs. Alice Snitzer Burke, of New York,
and Miss Nell Richardson, of Hagerstown Maryland, arrived in the
city yesterday on its way to New York, where the much-heralded
transcontinental run for suffrage will end next Saturday.

When the little car chug-chugged up to the North Water St.
corner of Main street, where an open-air suffragist meeting was held
yesterday afternoon, the meter registered 10,158 miles, which isn't
half bad for a little car—or for a big car.

Mrs. Burke and Miss Richardson left New York on April 6th
with the idea of making a trip along the border of the United States.
Except that they did not touch Florida and that they were driven
from the south to the north of Texas because of the chaotic conditions along the Mexican frontier, they have done so far just what
they sent out to-day. Also they have banged away for equal suffrage
at every place at which they have stopped, until they believe they
have really convinced several thousands of men that to give votes
for women is the only way to play the game "on the level."

SMALL, BUT IT GETS THERE.

The little car that the trip has been made in isn't even as large as
the one about which books of jokes have been compiled. It is low
and short and light. It has four wheels, however, a sturdy engine
and two indomitable passengers who believe that bad roads and
blow-outs shouldn't be considered in the promulgation of the great
idea of equal suffrage.

Each and every time the little car stops, even though it be to
repair a puncture or to take on oil or gasoline, there is a suffrage talk.
It may be in the heart of a great city or it may be in a quiet village

street where a few store loungers gather. The cause of equal suffrage is omnipresent with the two women motorists. The car which is yellow and covered with names of persons and towns, is a better drawing card than a brass band and once a crowd is around it one of the women mounts the seat and talks—talks votes for women.

HAD SOME ROUGH RIDING

"Next to equal suffrage, the one thing I would like to advocate is good roads," said Mrs. Burke to a reporter yesterday afternoon. "We know good roads, and, let me tell you, we have become intimately acquainted with a great number of bad roads. In the South and the West we struck roads with ruts in them so large that little car would almost get lost. We were on the Lincoln highway once, in Ohio, and it was a terrible stretch of road. I think when I am through with this trip I shall take the stump for good roads. Somebody should."

Mrs. Burke, who does all the driving on the trip, says she and Miss Richardson have not had one accident since they left New York. They have had very little car trouble, and, despite the roads encountered, relatively little tire trouble. The single unpleasant personal experience that they had was in a town in Louisiana where they had difficulty with a drunken crowd.

CARGO INCLUDES A CAT

Although their car is one of the smallest of the better-known small cars, Mrs. Burke and Miss Richardson have managed to carry an entire wardrobe, including evening dresses, cooking outfit, a typewriter, a few books, and a cat. On the right front fender of the machine is a "luck dog," carved by a Japanese woman, which was given to them in San Francisco. On the other front fender is a set of Elk's horns, a gift from an old Western pioneer. When the little yellow car bowled up Main Street yesterday it was decorated with golden rod and two or three yellow streamers, for yellow, lest you have forgotten, is the suffragists' color.

"What, besides bad roads, have you learned to dislike since you started on your trip?" Mrs. Burke was asked.

"Brilliant headlights," she promptly answered. "Of all the abominable things that you met on the roads, they are the worst. The ordinary driver doesn't dim them and it is impossible to drive into them and be safe. You can't prohibit the sale of them, so long as they are manufactured, but I honestly believe the men who make them should be prosecuted."

ALWAYS CORDIALLY RECEIVED

Mrs. Burke said that she and Miss Richardson were cordially received wherever they went. In the states that have not yet granted equal suffrage their reception was more enthusiastic than in those in which the vote has been given to women. The Southern and the Western people were particularly enthusiastic over the Golden Flier and its passengers. At San Jose, Cal., a band and scores of automobiles met the "flier" and escorted it into the city. Governors of states, mayors and other officeholders frequently received the two women.

Mrs. Burke was an experienced motorist before she attempted the trip. In the suffrage campaign of 1915 she toured New York state in a car. She is able to change tires, make repairs to broken parts of the car and remedy the engine's disorders.

Mrs. Burke and Miss Richardson will remain in this city today and leave tomorrow for Syracuse. They journeyed from Buffalo yesterday, which is a little short of their daily average of 100 miles.[114]

DAY 173: MONDAY, SEPTEMBER 25, 1916
ROCHESTER TO SYRACUSE, NY
APPROXIMATELY 10,245 MILES TRAVELED

DAY 174: TUESDAY, SEPTEMBER 26, 1916
SYRACUSE TO UTICA TO ILION, NY
APPROXIMATELY 10,345 MILES TRAVELED

DAY 175: WEDNESDAY, SEPTEMBER 27, 1916
ILION TO KINGSTON, NY
APPROXIMATELY 10,500 MILES TRAVELED

New York Tribune
SUFFRAGE AUTO IS DUE SATURDAY.
"YELLOW BABY" AND WOMEN TOURISTS
WINDING UP 35,000-MILE TRIP.

With a record of 35,000 miles for suffrage behind it, the plucky little Golden Flier, which has carried two women and fourteen suffrage speeches will come honking home again next Saturday afternoon.

The returned Prodigal's reception wasn't in it with the one the suffragists are going to give their "Yellow Baby." Banners will fly, bugles will blow and thirty autoloads of women will wave flags when the Woman Suffrage party led by its chairman Miss Mary Garrett Hay turns out to greet Mrs. Alice Snitjer Burke and Miss Nell Richardson, back from hard-fought fields. Since Mrs. Carrie Chapman Catt, national chairman, christened the Golden Flier with a bottle of gasolene, it has bumped into Jersey mules, through Virginia mud and over Colorado mountains, until it has visited every state in the union except those of New England.

Mrs. Burke and Miss Richardson left New York with two evening gowns and seven suffrage speeches apiece, a fireless cooker, a small store of provisions, a mutual scorn for tramps and boundless faith in the cause. They are coming back with all of them—except the store of provisions—in spite of snowstorms and spring freshets and desert winds, endured for suffrage.

The formal welcome to the wanderers will take place at the city line at Broadway and West 263d Street on Saturday, at 1:30 P.M., from which point the Golden Flier will be escorted in state to the headquarters of the Woman's Suffrage party, at 48 East Thirty-fourth Street. Here a reception will be held at 3:30 p.m. and while tea is being served prominent suffrage speakers will eulogize the Votes for Women tourists.

Among the speakers will be Miss Mary Garrett Hay, Mrs. Carrie Chapman Catt, Mrs. Norman de R. Whitehouse, chairman of the Woman Suffrage party of New York state; Miss Annie Doughty, chairman of Manhattan Borough, and Mrs. B. C. Howard, leader of the 17th Assembly District.

Mrs. J. L. McCutcheon, chairman of the committee in charge of the welcome-home exercises, has planned for the automobiles to be decorated with big yellow rosettes and streamers of yellow, white and blue as they leave the suffrage headquarters at 12 o'clock. Four women buglers will ride in advance, and prominent women from the Assembly district will fill the cars. The boroughs of Queens, Richmond, The Bronx and Brooklyn will be represented, as well as that of Manhattan.[115]

Kingston Daily Freeman
LITTLE YELLOW CAR RAMBLES INTO TOWN.
Mrs. Alice Snitzer [sic] Burke of New York, Miss Nell Richardson of Winchester, Virginia and "Saxon" a coal black kitten arrived in Kingston on Wednesday and while in town are the guests of Mrs. M.J. Michael. Mrs. Burke and Miss Richardson and "Saxon," the kitten, are on the last lap of a tour which included a visit to the four corners of the United States. The entire trip has been made in a little yellow Saxon runabout and to date 10,500 miles have been completed. According to the schedule laid down when the trio left New York on April 6, the trip was to include a complete circuit of the United States and was to end at New York on Saturday, September 30, less than six months after the start and the most remarkable part of the trip is that the schedule has been maintained and entire trip was made with the two suffragettes at the wheel and "Saxon" the cat perched upon the radiator or sleeping on top of the car.

The little yellow Saxon attracts hundreds of visitors in every city where they have stopped and at Ilion while the occupants were at lunch an officer was stationed in the car to keep off the throng which crowded around. A meeting will be held this evening at the corner of John and Fair street when Mrs. Burke and Miss Richardson will speak from the car in the interest of suffrage.

The coast to coast trip was a begun on April 6, going south to Atlanta, Ga, then west through Texas and across the Arizona desert to San Diego, then north through California to Seattle and back through Montana and the Dakotas and the trip will end Saturday at 1:30 at New York city. The entire trip was made alone and covers in the neighborhood of 11,000 miles.

While on the Mexican border about the time of the mobilization of troops there the little yellow car and occupants traveled sometimes for an entire day without seeing a native other than the Mexicans who roam about. During the entire trip they were never molested however although at times they were near where raids occurred.

Four mountain ranges were crossed by the little car, and many a time the car was fast for hours in deep mud and sand but during the entire trip no mechanical trouble was experienced. Mrs. Burke makes a daily inspection of the car and takes entire care of the car. This morning before leaving the Central Garage, where the car was left during the night, Mrs. Burke was found filling oil cups and making minor adjustments to the car. Mr. Kennedy, proprietor of the Central, is the local agent for the Saxon cars.

In every state visited speeches in the interest of suffrage were made. Three weeks were spent in Texas, five weeks in California and two weeks in South Dakota. Friday a stop will be made in Pough-keepsie which is the last stop until New York is reached on Saturday.

The car is covered with names which [have] been scratched in the paint and the seat covers are black with the thousands of names of visitors along the route. On the hood of the car some enthusiastic booster of the west has painted, "Spokane, the best city," while boosters of other cities along the route had painted the names of their own town upon the car.

Shovels, spare tires, rope, desert water bags, a typewriter and during the western trip a sewing machine was a part of the baggage carried. Every available space has been utilized for spare parts, still the only trouble experienced was spring trouble in the rough mountain roads in the west.

Attached to one of the front lamps is an elk's horn presented by a pioneer of the west and attached to the rear of the top is a big yellow key 3 feet long presented by the mayor of San Jose, bearing the words, "Votes for Women." The skin of a snake which was killed by being run over on the western desert is draped over the back of the car.

During the entire trip the best roads were experienced in New York state and California although for long stretches other states have begun improving the highways.

Both women are representing the National American Suffrage Association of which Mrs. Carrie Chapman Catt is president.

The route as laid out with the dates of the arrival dates appear in the door of the car as follows: New York, April 6, 1916; New Orleans, April 27; Los Angeles, June 4; San Francisco, June 14;

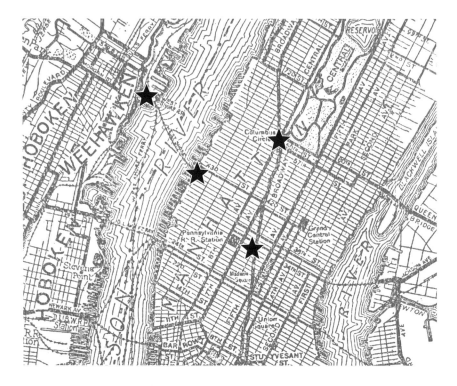

HOME AGAIN IN NEW YORK CiTY

DAY 178: SATURDAY, SEPTEMBER 30, 1916
POUGHKEEPSIE TO NEW YORK CITY
APPROXIMATELY 10,700 MILES TRAVELED

New York Tribune
**BROADWAY HAILS SUFFRAGE AUTO INTREPID
WOMEN DRIVERS AND 10,700 MILE JOURNEY.**
BULLETS AND RIVER HELD NO TERRORS. MUD AND DUST
OF THIRTY-SIX STATES MARK LITTLE GOLDEN FLYER.
Lost four days in the Arizona desert, shot at on the Mexican border,
twenty-four hours without water, stuck in six feet of Washington
snow, losing an axle in the waters of the Oregon—and all for Votes
for Women!

It sounds just like a motion picture scenario, and a particularly
dizzy one at that, but is the actual experience of two young women of
New York, Mrs. Alice Snitjer Burke and Miss Nell Richardson, who
honked gallantly down Fifth Avenue [Saturday] in the little yellow

suffrage car, the "Golden Flier," which has carried them 17,000 miles since April 6. With the mud and dust of thirty-six states on their tires, a deer's antler from the distant West on the back of their car, a twenty-four-inch key to San Jose extending askew over the edge, and their "lucky dog" and their "cat-o'-nine-tails" still on the job, the dauntless suffragists returned.

The cat-o'-nine-tails deserves a paragraph all to himself, for it was through his sleeping basket that the Mexican bullet went, one day when the two motorists had left their car for repairs while they went on a short trip by train along the border. As a matter of fact, Saxon has only one tail, but he got his name from the fact that he is a rah-rah-rah cat and a suffrage mascot.

Cat Got the Last Drop

It was Saxon who got the last drop of water when Mrs. Burke and Miss Richardson were lost in the Arizona desert between Phoenix and Yuma. Saxon got more headlines in the newspaper clear across the continent than the suffragists themselves did. He joined the party as a frisky kitten in New Jersey, but yesterday a staid cat came back, a witness of arduous labors performed and dangers endured for suffrage.

Fifteen automobiles full of cheering suffragists met the tiny yellow car that had circled every state in the Union except the New England ones yesterday afternoon at Broadway and 263d Street. Four girl buglers led the way in the triumphal file back to the headquarters of the New York Woman Suffrage Party. Flags waved and yellow pennants fluttered, and the small boys all the way down Broadway and Riverside Drive and clear across town to Fifth Avenue set up a shrill shout to help things along.

"It's the suffragettes," the boys said which showed that even the New York male is being educated up to the fact that there is such a thing as votes for women.

A negro driver in an automobile truck stood up in his seat at Broadway and Ninety-sixth Street and yelled out "God bless de suffragettes and God save de men!" His meaning seemed a little ambiguous, and the welcoming party didn't quite know whether to be flattered or not.

Suffrage Car Stalls

At Broadway and Fifty-seventh Street the car in which Mrs. Edward F. Taylor and Mrs. David Rogers, district leaders, were driving got stuck. Nothing could budge it until the women got out and pushed, giving a practical illustration of the resourcefulness of suffragists.

There was another triumphal procession at 48 East Thirty-fourth Street, headquarters of the Woman Suffrage Party, where Miss Mary Garrett Hay, state chairman, Dr. Katherine Bement Davis, and a long line of borough chairmen and other suffrage leaders stood waiting to welcome the wanderers home. It was Saxon, though, who got the chief ovation of the afternoon and purred contentedly through it. Saxon has been trained to hiss when the word "anti-suffragist" is mentioned, but never at any other time, the motorists said.

Miss May welcomed the suffrage adventurers back, in the name of the Woman Suffrage Party. Dr. Davis said that they had forever freed their sex from the charge of being afraid of mice by their courageous trip through deserts and over mountains, in the interest of suffrage. Mrs. Fred Schuyler, of Buffalo; Mrs. Martha W. Suffern, of New York; Miss Annie Doughty, Mrs. Rogers and Miss Howard also made brief speeches of welcome.

Dr. Davis introduced a bit of spice into the afternoon, when she insisted upon telling the non-partisan suffragists why she intends to go out on the Hughes train on Monday. She said that she was going to talk for suffrage all the way.

Miss Richardson and Mrs. Burke told of their travels, while the suffragists listened breathlessly and Saxon purred, in token that it was all true. Then travellers, [sic] reception committee and guests adjourned to the tea room to eat the huge yellow cake adorned with kewpie suffragists sent by the 17th District, in which both the motorists live.

Miss Emily Hooper, leader of the 5th District; Miss Amy Lewis its treasurer, and Miss Gladys Silver suddenly disclosed a rival cake, which wasn't as large nor quite so yellow, but was exactly as good, they declared. And it is a matter of solemn record that Saxon ate seven slices.[117]

AFTERWORD

Alice Burke

On News Years Eve, as 1894 was turning to 1895, Alice Snitjer, 18, married Charles Albert Armstrong in San Jose, California. Seventeen months later, their daughter Bonney was born and two years later, Charles was dead in Florida, struck down by influenza he may have contracted in Cuba while serving with Teddy Roosevelt's Rough Riders. Two years to the day from Charles' death, Alice married Richard Burke, a doctor 16 years her senior and tennis partner of her mother. A year later, Richard, too, was dead. Alice, dismayed to find she had to share Richard's insurance policy with his nieces and nephews, moved with her daughter back into her parents' home.

Apparently Alice had higher ambitions than being "just" a wife or a mother. By 1910, Alice, 33, had moved to New York City, leaving Bonney, age 14, in San Jose to be raised by her mother. Activism was calling her.

Alice's first appearance in the *New York Times* was September 22, 1912, when she was reported to be selling pins and distributing literature for Teddy Roosevelt's Progressive Party, also known as the Bull Moose party. A year later, Alice was involved with a tiny Suffragist grocery store facing Broadway near Ninety-fifth Street. With her was Aimee Hutchinson, who had been dismissed from her teaching position when she dared to march in a 1912 suffrage parade. The Suffrage Pure Food Shop Company's window was filled with yellow pennants proclaiming the "Women Should Vote." The soda fountain inside supplied patrons with "sanitary" drinking cups. The discussions were about pure food and the vote. Upton Sinclair bought whole wheat and brown rice from them.

Alice's evening "soap box speeches" became famous. When asked how she got started, Alice replied:

"I was standing on a corner turning over sheets on which were printed suffrage arguments when a man in the crowd said something about the English militants. Something within me pushed right back on that soap box and I answered that man and talked for an hour. My friends were surprised and so was I. That incident gave me the confidence I lacked and I certainly have done some speaking since. Why right out on the corner of Ninety-sixth street and Broadway I spoke 165 nights from my little soap box. I didn't want to be confined to one district, so I resigned from the woman suffrage party and "freelanced," that is, I went where I pleased, into the theatre district, into Wall Street, any place where I thought I could push along the Cause for the vote.

"I suppose I must have looked odd, for every evening I would take my little soap box under my arm and march down into the subway and go to my meeting place. The passengers looked askance at me, but even that aided the cause. It drew attention to equal suffrage, and made men and women think."[118]

Eleven days after the welcome back to New York party, Alice was back in the midwest as part of the the Hughes Alliance Party. She took the train.

Alice returned to California sometime before 1940 and died there in 1948.

Nell Richardson

Nell Byron Richardson was born on 2 May 1890, to Hugh Richardson and Anne Kiger in Winchester, Virginia. By 1900, Nell's family had moved to Hagerstown, Maryland. Little is known about her early life. She moved to New York City around 1913 and by June 1, 1915, was living with Alice Burke as a lodger.[119] While in Manhattan, she was the Organizing Secretary for the New York Party (NAWSA, the National American Woman Suffrage Association).[120]

On December 27, 1916, Nell married Winthrop Randall Howard in Ohio. By 1920 she and her husband were living on Long Island, New York. They had a son, Winthrop, in 1924. In 1928 Nell Howard married Bruce Hoggson. Census records show her living in Washington, DC, and St. Louis, MO.

Nell died in Maryland at the end of December 1949. She is buried in Baltimore. Little else is known at this point.

Acknowledgments

Researching Alice and Nell's ride has been a long process. As I've lived with these women in my brain for years, I have also subjected my family and friends to endless talk about what the ladies were thinking. Where were they then?

It is with gratitude and love that I want to thank my family first. The Moors gang have rolled their eyes more than once I am sure. To Cristine, Marcel, Camellia and Camden: thank you so much for your interest, support, and theories. It feels so good to have a cheering section and you all are the best. To my son, Jeff Shauger, who dove into the project head first, researching, reading endless newspaper articles, and finding gems among the words. Thank you for all your enthusiasm and your endless offers of help. And to my husband, Alex Huppé who started this project with his love for old cars. What a ride. I love you all.

A big thank you too to Seal Cove Auto Museum on Mount Desert Island, Maine, for putting the Golden Flyer front and center, telling the story of these remarkable women to adults and children alike.

And thank you too to Phil Zuckerman who wandered into Seal Cove one day and said to the curator, Bill Barter, that the story of Alice and Nell was worthy of a book. Bill said, call Jeryl.

Notes

1 The Golden Flier is often spelled "Flier" as well as "Flyer." The spellings were historically interchangeable.
2 "Suffrage Flier Speeds on Way." New York Tribune, 7 April 1916, 5
3 "'The Yellow Kid' on Its Cross Continental Run." Kansas City Star (Kansas City, MO), 12 April 1916, 20
4 "Suffrage Flier Speeds on Way." New York Tribune, 7 April 1916, 5
5 "Suffrage Flier Speeds on Way." New York Tribune, 7 April 1916, 5
6 Burke, Alice. "Diary of the Golden Flier." Boston Daily Globe, 19 April 1916, 11
7 "Golden Flyer Flying." Gettysburg Compiler, 29 April 1916.
8 "Women on 15,000-Mile Vote Campaign Reach Here." Philadelphia Inquirer, 8 April 1916, 12
9 "2 Suffrage Crusaders and Cat Mascot Aboard Yellow Car Here Today," New Orleans States, 28 April 1916, 4
10 Burke, Alice. "Diary of the Golden Flier." Boston Daily Globe, 19 April 1916, 11
11 "Golden Flyer Chugs In: Suffrage Missionaries Undaunted by the Storm. League's New Home Warmed." Baltimore Sun, 9 April 1916, 16
12 Burke, Alice. "Diary of the Golden Flier." Boston Daily Globe, 19 April 1916, 11
13 Burke, Alice. "Diary of the Golden Flier." Boston Daily Globe, 19 April 1916, 11
14 "Nation-wide Interest Shown in the Tour of Alice Snitjer Burke." San Jose Mercury News (San Jose, CA), 23 April 1916, 28
15 "Nation-wide Interest Shown in the Tour of Alice Snitjer Burke." San Jose Mercury News (San Jose, CA), 23 April 1916, 28
16 Burke, Alice. "Diary of the Golden Flier." Boston Daily Globe, 22 April 1916, 11
17 "Nation-wide Interest Shown in the Tour of Alice Snitjer Burke." San Jose Mercury News (San Jose, CA), 23 April 1916, 28
18 Burke, Alice. "Diary of the Golden Flier." Boston Daily Globe, 22 April 1916, 11
19 "In Raleigh." Everything (Greensboro, NC), 22 Apr 1916, 11
20 Burke, Alice. "Diary of the Golden Flier." Boston Daily Globe, 22 April 1916, 11
21 Ibid.
22 Ibid.
23 "Golden Flier Startles South." New York Tribune, 2 May 1916, 8
24 "Social Chat." Augusta Chronicle (Augusta, GA), 16 April 1916, 17
25 Burke, Alice. "Diary of the Golden Flier." Boston Daily Globe, 2 May 1916, 9
26 Ibid.
27 Ibid.
28 "Golden Flyer in Alabama." Birmingham News (Birmingham, AL), 23 April 1916, 20
29 Ibid.
30 "Noted Suffragists Carry Dresses and Typewriter in Yellow 'Baby Saxon'" Montgomery Advertiser (Montgomery, AL), 23 April 1916, 26
31 "Flier Survives Dixie Highways." New York Tribune, 14 May 1916, 15
32 Ibid.
33 Ibid.
34 "2 Suffrage Crusaders and Cat Mascot Aboard Yellow Car Here Today." New Orleans States, 28 April 1916, 4
35 "Flier Survives Dixie Highways." New York Tribune, 14 May 1916, 15
36 "Yellow Roadster Rostrum of Suffragists,"State Times Advocate (Baton Rouge, LA), 29 April 1916, 8
37 Ibid.
38 "Flier Survives Dixie Highways." New York Tribune, 14 May 1916, 15
39 Ibid.
40 "Suffrage Tourists Arrive." Houston Post, 4 May 1916, 8
41 "'Golden Flyer' in Texas Sun, Carries Message of Suffrage." New York Tribune, 29 May 1916, 7

42   Ibid.
43   Ibid.
44   Ibid.
45   "Couriers of Suffrage Spoke to Large Crowd." Houston Post, 9 May 1916, 11
46   "'Golden Flyer' In Texas Sun, Carries Message of Suffrage." New York Tribune, 29 May 1916, 7
47   "'Votes for Women' Car Reaches Dallas." Dallas Morning News (Dallas, TX), 11 May 1916, 6
48   'Golden Flyer' in Texas Sun, Carries Message of Suffrage." New York Tribune, 29 May 1916, 7
49   "Suffrage Auto Fails to Come." El Paso Herald (El Paso, TX), 13 May 1916, 5
50   "'Golden Flyer' in Border Towns." New York Tribune, 4 June 1916, 7
51   Ibid.
52   Ibid.
53   Ibid.
54   "Look for 'Golden Flier.'" El Paso Herald (El Paso, TX), 20 May 1916, 18
55   "Saxons Have Part In Villa Chase." Evening Capital News (Boise, ID), 10 April 1916, 11
56   "Suffragets Here In Car." El Paso Herald (El Paso, TX), 22 May 1916, 4
57   "Vote Hunters Have A Thrill." El Paso Herald, (El Paso, TX), 27 May 1916, 21
58   "'Golden Flyer' in Border Towns." New York Tribune, 4 June 1916. 7
59   Burke, Alice. "Suffragist's Jabs at the Man Made Laws." El Paso Herald, (El Paso, TX), 23 May 1916, 6
60   "Suffrage Leader Takes Rap At Mere." El Paso Times (El Paso, TX), 24 May 1916, 10
61   "Women on Tour Find Dry Gains", Detroit Times, (Detroit, MI), 16 September 1916, 1
62   Arizona Daily Star (Tucson, AZ), 28 May 1916, page 9
63   "Golden Flyer Bears Pair of Plucky Suffragists." Arizona Republican (Phoenix, AZ), 28 May 28, 1916, 8
64   "Women On Tour Find Dry Gains." Detroit Times, 16 September 1916, 1
65   "Golden Flier Due Thursday." Evening Tribune (San Diego, CA), 31 May 1916, 8
66   "Famous Women Motorists Arrive." Oakland Tribune (Oakland, CA), 18 June 1916, 40
67   "Suffrage Workers Reach Portland." Oregon Daily Journal (Portland, Multnomah, OR), 9 July 1916, 4
68   "Two Suffrage Women in Little Yellow Car." Anaconda Standard (Anaconda, MT), 31 July 1916, 5
69   "They're Not Lost." Los Angeles Times, 1 June 1916, 10
70   "Golden Flier Suffragists Visit Fair." San Diego Union (San Diego, CA), 8 June 1916, 7
71   "Personalities." Coronado Strand (Coronado, CA), 10 June 1916, 3
72   "The City and Environs." Los Angeles Times, 5 June 1916, 10
73   "Spreading The Gospel of 'Votes For Women'." Los Angeles Times, 7 June 1916, 22
74   "New York Visitor." Modesto Evening News (Modesto, CA), 9 June 1916, 3
75   "Local Suffragists To Give Public Reception." San Jose Mercury News (San Jose, CA), 8 June 1916, 7
76   "Suffragists Tell Of Cross Country Drive." San Jose Mercury (San Jose, CA), 14 June 1916, 5
77   "Famous Women Motorists Arrive." Oakland Tribune (Oakland, CA), 18 June 1916, 40
78   "A Suffrage Leader." Riverside Independent Enterprise (Riverside, CA), 14 June 1916, 2
79   "Suffragists Flit In And Then Out Of Berkeley." Oakland Tribune (Oakland, CA), 28 June 1916, 1
80   Sacramento Bee (Sacramento, CA), 1 July 1916, 5
81   "Women On Motor Tour Around Border Of US." Morning Register (Eugene, OR), 7 July 1916, 7
82   "Hope Lies In West." Oregonian (Portland, OR), 9 July 1916, 15
83   "Eastern Suffragists Continue Tour in Fight for Ballot." Oregon Daily Journal (Portland, OR), 12 July 1916, 15
84   "Votes Are Pledged." Oregonian (Portland, OR), 10 July 1916, 10
85   "Suffragists Are To Leave Today." Oregonian (Portland, OR), 12 July 1916, 4
86   "Local Suffs Await Yellow Auto." Seattle Star, 14 July 1916, 10
87   "'Suffs' To Speak Saturday To Club." Seattle Star, 14 July 1916, 2
88   "Look For Suffrage Auto." Spokane Chronicle (Spokane, WA), 19 July 1916, 3
89   "Women On Tour Of U.S. In Auto." Spokesman-Review (Spokane, WA), 22 July 1916, 10

90 "Women On Tour Find Dry Gains." Detroit Times, 16 September 1916, 1

91 "Women On Tour Find Dry Gains." Detroit Times, 16 September 1916, 1

92 "Lady Suffragists Make Missoula on Tour." Missoulian (Missoula, MT), 28 July, 1916 1916, 2

93 "Two Suffrage Women in Little Yellow Car." Anaconda Standard (Anaconda, MT), 31 July 1916, 5

94 "Visitors Travel 7000 Miles For Suffrage." Butte Miner (Butte, MT), 31 July 1916, 5.

95 "Record Auto Trip By Woman Tourist." Anaconda Standard (Anaconda, MT), 12 Oct 1916, 9

96 "Little 'Yellow Car' At Redfield." Aberdeen American (Aberdeen, TX), 18 August1916, 5

97 "The Golden Flier is in Huron." Huron Daily Huronite (Huron, SD), 16 August 1916, 1

98 "Yellow Car Caught In Rain." Huron Daily Huronite (Huron, SD), 21 August1916, 1

99 Ibid.

100 "Local Notes." Mitchell Capital (Mitchell, SD), 24 August1916, 3

101 "Society Notes." Argus-Leader (Sioux Falls, SD), 23 August1916, 8

102 Burke, Alice, "Letter to the Editor."Argus-Leader (Sioux Falls, SD), 26 August1916, 10

103 Argus-Leader (Sioux Falls, SD), 28 August 1916, 5

104 Ibid.

105 "What Some Women Are Doing." Motor Age, Vol. 30, October 1916, 28

106 "Political Equality Club To Have Charge Of Suffrage Booth Today At State Fair." Star Tribune (Minneapolis, MN), 4 September 1916, 5

107 La Crosse Tribune (La Crosse, WI), 9 September 1916, 6

108 "'Golden Flier' Suffrage Car In Madison On Longest Tour." Wisconsin State Journal (Madison, WI), 11 September 1916, 5

109 "Special Car for Suffs." Chicago Tribune (Chicago, IL), 13 September 1916, 3

110 "Covering National in Saxon Working for Suffrage for Women." South Bend News-Times (South Bend, IN), 18 Sepember 1916, 2

111 "Suffragists Travel 6,500 Miles In Auto." Grand Rapids Press (Grand Rapids, MI), 15 September 1916, 22

112 "Mrs. Burke Won't talk Politics." Detroit Free Press, 17 September 1916, 6

113 "Little Yellow Car." Buffalo Morning Express and Illustrated Buffalo Express (Buffalo, NY), 22 September 1916, 9

114 "Never Too Badly Bumped To Talk." Democrat and Chronicle (Rochester, NY), 24 September 1916, 23

115 "Suffrage Auto Is Due Saturday." New York Tribune, 27 September 1916, 9

116 "Little Yellow Car Rambles Into Town." Kingston Daily Freeman (Kingston, NY), 28 September 1916, 5

117 "Broadway Hails Suffrage Auto." New York Tribune (New York, NY), 1 October 1916, 13

118 "San Jose Woman Wins Fame in the Suffrage Cause in the East." San Jose Mercury News (San Jose, CA),18 July 1915, 5

119 "New York, State Census, 1915," index, FamilySearch (https://familysearch.org/pal:/MM9.1.1/K923-JRV : accessed 19 Mar 2014), Nellie Richardson, New York, New York, New York, United States; from "New York, State Census, 1915," index and images, Ancestry.com (www.ancestry.com : 2012); citing state population census schedules, 1915, p. 07, line 43, New York State Archives, Albany

120 "Winchester Girl Campaigns for Suffragists." Winchester Evening Star (Winchester, VA), 8 Apr 1916.